Practical VAASTUSHASTRA

Practical
VAASTUSHASHTRA

Acharya Satyanand

Diamond Pocket Books (P) Ltd.
X-30, Okhla Industrial Area, Phase-2
New Delhi-110 020

Publisher	:	**Diamond Pocket Books (P) Ltd.**
		X-30, Okhla Industrial Area, Phase-II
		New Delhi-110020
Phone	:	011-40712200
E-mail	:	wecare@diamondbooks.in
Website	:	www.diamondbooks.in
Edition	:	2025
Printed by	:	Repro (India)

Practical Vastushastra
By : Acharya Satyanand

CONTENTS

GRATITUDE

Due to the encouragement and popularity enjoyed by our Hindi & Bengali versions of 'Practical Vaastushastra', we feel privileged to offer English version thereof to our learned readers.

We have incorporated only the very Practical aspects of Vaastu, keeping in mind that it is entertaining, in addition to relevant knowledge, and the concepts explained can easily be applied in day-to-day living. Your letters are indicative of the success of our effort.

In the end, we are grateful to Mr. Suresh Chandra Jain of Calcutta who has inspired me to writing. Last, but not the least, we express our heartily gratitude to the Managing Director of Diamond Pocket Books, Mr.Narendra Kumar who, with all his zeal, has brought out this esteemed publication in a beautiful form conveying the much needed information to the valued readers.

Acharya Satyanand
Smt. Jayashree

1.1.97

Loknath Bhawan
Irabati Pally,
Kazipara, Barasat,
24, Parganas (N) W.B.
Ph: 033-5526012

Origin of Vaastu

The Universe—The world is created by the five elements viz Earth, Fire, Air, Water and Sky.

All these five elements are inanimate elements whereas human being is a living being. Whatever or whichever work is done, whether the work is small or big, these five elements act as the catalyst-medium for the work done.

All these five elements are natural. Among the living creatures, the human being enjoys high superior category. Man, with his glory and lusture and with vast intelligence, had adjusted these five elements in such a way that he had made the modern world gorgeous, rich and sophisticated.

But whenever man misused natural virtues of these five elements he had to face many problems like accidents, sufferings, pain, bad results, sadness etc.

If a man leads a life in accordance with the laws of nature, then a man lives a healthy and long life, also obeying the laws of the Vaastu Shastra, the nature gives us immense happiness.

Our ancestors had vast knowledge on the subject of vaastu. Our holy books, Ramayan and Mahabharat, are the best example of this fact. Our old temples, buildings, palaces and big towers are some of the unique examples of the vaastu art. Therefore we can say that living according to the nature is the Vaastu Shastra and the cause of origin of vaastu depends upon this fact only.

The people living in the building obey all the laws and rules of vaastu and are always religious, rich and healthy [free of any deadly disease]. The laws and principles of the vaastu theory are in conformity with the scientific viewpoint. This theory holds back a very solid scientific base.

The whole Vaastu Shastra depends upon the law of Nature. The North pole and the South pole of the earth has magnetic property, thus same way in the man, the upper portion of the head is called North pole and the lower portion of the leg is called South pole.

The flow of the Magnetic force is always from the North pole to the South pole. According to the Magnetic property there is always repulsion in the North to North and South to South pole. Special attention is given to these properties of Man and earth in the Vaastu Shastra.

Besides this the earth has its own gravitation due to which it attracts all the things and objects towards itself. This gravitational force is alike for the non living and living beings.

The most important thing, in the Vaastu Shastra, is that there is no word called lifeless in the Vaastu. Today the modern science also accepts this viewpoint that the last particle of the matter is an atom.

After doing the analysis we have seen that in every atom the properties of matter is electron, proton and neutron. According to the nature these electron, proton and neutron are always mobile . Out of these three, one is stable and the other two keep rotating in their range. When the last particle of an atom of a non-living object is mobile then how could it be a dead thing? In light of this natural miracle the science is silent on all such aspects. The most dangerous bomb, the atom bomb, is made by just changing the numbers of the last rotating particle. The whole formula of making atom bomb is based on this principle only. Therefore, we should behave according to the property and trait of the matter.

The origin of Vaastu and Vaastu Shastra emanates from the said revelations. In vaastu shastra the rotation of earth is from west to the east direction and it also holds an important place. We see the rising of sun from the east and setting in the west. This is due to the rotation of earth, from west to east direction. Alongwith this the Earth is inclined on its axis at the angle of 23 1/ 2°.

The state of the earth's Vaastu-Shastra is based upon the situation of Sun, the property and the position of the matter. Everybody knows that the Sun-rays in the morning, are blessing and boon for the living beings but due to their radio-active substance, are harmful and hazardous also.

There is a beautiful example of Vaastu Shastra in the Vaastu mala.

Striputradi Bhogsaur Vyajanam dharmmarthKampradam!
Jantunamyanm Sukhaspadamidam shitambudharmapadam!!
Vapi dewegrahadi punyamKhitam gehatsamutupadhyte!
Geham purbhashantiten vinudha shri wiswakarmadyh!!

(Vaastu mala)

The happiness and desire of woman, child, son, religion, work, purpose of existence of man is controlled by the planet which also saves the man from cold, hot and wind. According to the law, the man making the house, gets the virtue and blessings for making well and temple. Therefore, the Vishwakarma, The Holy architect, had given the order to make the house first.

Amartyashchaiva martyasheh yatra-yatra wasanti hi
Tad wa sitwati matam tajshestdabhedam cha wadamyaham!!
Bhumi prasadayanani shayanam cha chaturvidham!
Prasadadini vaastuni vaastutwad vaastu sanshrayat
Vaastu hi lanyaw proktanyasmin puratneh

(May)

Which means, now, I describe various divisions of vaastu-science which is dear to men and gods alike. Land, building, eating and living pattern and sleep are four sub-divisions of vaastu-science, of which land is upper-most. Other facets are also adorned by vaastu. Now I dwell upon facets of vaastu-shastra which was followed by our ancient seers.

In recent times, work on building construction is done by architects but architecture and vaastu are not identical.

The whole concept of this vaastu mala is that human beings and God live where there is the vaastu science and its secrets.

Vaastu has four constituents : Earth (Bhumi),residence, status, and position of sleeping, of which Earth is the main constituent. Relating to the earth there are other parts. Prasad vaastu shastra is ornamented by the vaastu-art. The sayings of holy men who researched the Vaastu Shastra is described here.

In the modern world the building of the house is done by the architect. but the architecture and the vaastu are not same. Architecture is an important science which is based upon the numbers and mathematics.

But vaastu is much larger than the Architecture. This is related with the religion and the literature. It is very vast and immense. Vaastu is said to be one of the oldest among the 64 Ancient literatures. Vaastu is not science but it is equivalent to the science.

Vaastu means the plot on which the house has to be built, should be carefully taken. The land surrounding the plot should be thoroughly seen, the area and the width of the land should be examined. To know the main and actual meaning of Vaastu Shastra we should have the knowledge of direction first.

There are 8 directions.

(1) EAST

(2) WEST

(3) NORTH

(4) SOUTH

(5) NORTH-EAST

(6) NORTH-WEST

(7) SOUTH-EAST

(8) SOUTH-WEST

The full account of these eight directions is given further.

Knowledge of Direction

To understand the Vaastu Shatra in a better way the knowledge of direction is very essential. Vaastu shastra is not limited to building a house only. To build a house, according to the vaastu, is very tough and complex job. The architect sees the plot and makes the plan of the area and builds the rooms according to your necèssity.

An Architect neither inspects the plot with the viewpoint of vaastu nor he examines the soil of the plot. He only sees the soil and makes the building on the plot. On the other hand a vaastu shastri never advices to buy the plot of land without examining the plot and the soil.

In the vaastu shastra the properties of the plot, the examination and research of the plot is done before constructing a house on the plot. After purchasing the plot the land has to be purified by holy mantras and law of entrance is very carefully observed.

The starting of vaastu shastra is done from the place from where the building has to be constructed. First of all, we should have correct and full knowledge of all the eight directions of the plot, on which the construction is to be done.

The knowledge of the directions is important from different and various types and methods. Untill we have correct knowledge of direction, we cannot have right idea about the nature of the plot. Therefore we can understand the directions from this figure easily:—

East, West, North, South are the four main directions. The middle

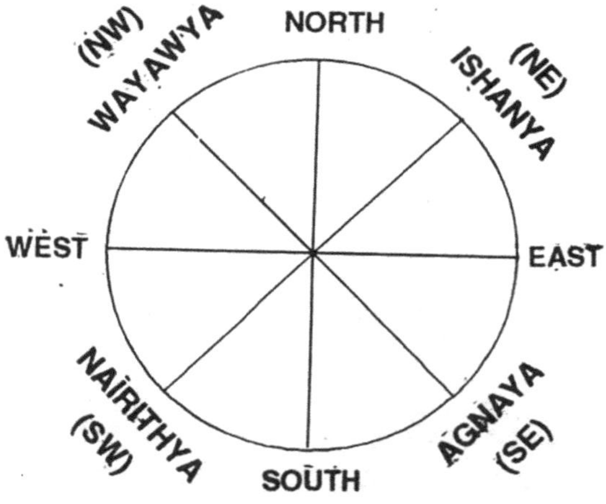

Figure No. 1

directions of these four directions are called co-sister direc.ions. They are also four.

(1) ISHAN—North east

(2) Wayava—North west

(3) Agnaya—South east

(4) Nairithya—South west

According to these four directions the plot can be divided into the

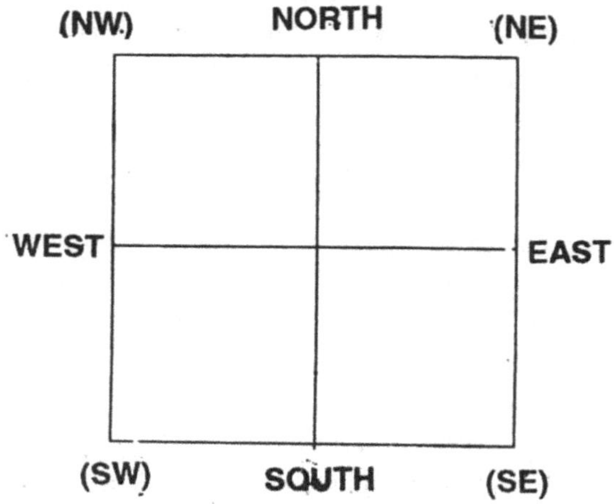

Figure No. 2

four parts, as follows.

(1) North East—Ishan Sector

(2) South East—Agnaya sector

(3) South west—Nairithya sector

(4) North West—Wayava sector

After dividing the plot into four parts, we divide it into eight parts, according to the eight directions. These eight directions are the life of vaastu shastra.

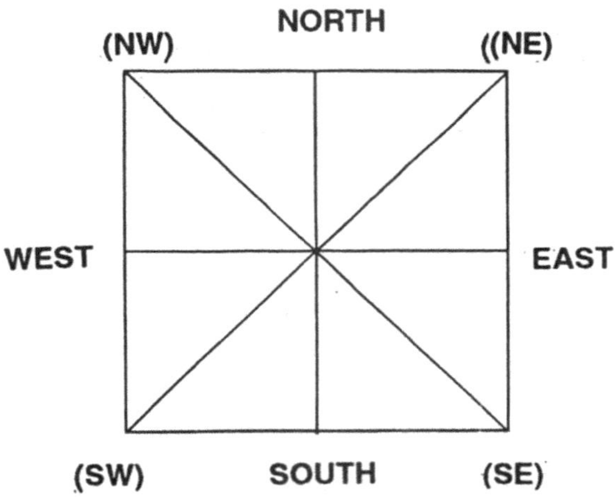

Figure No. 3

(1) North sector

(2) North east sector

(3) South sector

(4) South west sector

(5) East sector

(6) South east sector

(7) West sector

(8) North west sector.

IMPORTANCE OF EIGHT DIRECTIONS.

We should know the importance of the eight directions on which the whole vaastu shastra is based. Alongwith knowledge of direction, we should also know about the educational importance of the direction, because the vaastu shastra makes the rooms, verandah, bath rooms according to the knowledge of these directions.

(1) East direction is said to be the direction of family generation. Therefore, while constructing a house, we should leave some open area in the east direction. This gives a long life to the lord of the family.

(2) West direction gives success, glory, fame and fortune.

(3) North direction is the place of mother. By leaving open space in the North, maternal side profits.

(4) South direction has wealth, success, happiness and peace. Tirupati Mandir of India, made in the south, is thus an exemple of prosperity.

(5) North-East or Ishan sector should not have any type of fault or defect. This sector gives stability to the family.

(6) Wayava or North west sector is the cause of friendship and enmity. If you have fault in this sector, then you will have many enemies but, if it is faultless, then there will be lots of helpful friends.

(7) Agnaya or South-East sector is very hot, so it gives health to human beings. But the sector, having fault, makes the landlord very angry.

(8) Nairitaya or South-West gives birth to humble nature and good character. (If there is any defect in this sector, Land-lord may be in troubles).

DIRECTION & GOD

According to the Hindu religion man had bowed to the sun, because sun is deity and is the source of light and energy. Our ancient holy teachers, had made living houses for themselves, many thousand years ago, after analysing sun's rays only. Thus, the east facing houses are said to be the best house. Our ancestors knew that the ray of sun has life giving elements. Ancient people constructed thier houses, fully keeping in view the sun and sun-rays, as defined by the vaastu-shastra. So the factors, such as knowledge of direction, its importance and which direction is adorned by particular deity, should be kept in mind.

According to the shastra Gods reside in directions given below :—

Direction	—	**God**
North	—	Kuber, Som

South	—	Yam [God of death]
East	—	Indra & Sun
West	—	Varun
North east (Ishan)	—	Som & Shiva
South east (Agneya)	—	Bhrahma
South west (Nairitha)	—	Niriti
North west (Wayava)	—	Wayu.

The direction of the plot, which is square is easily understood. But most of the plots are not found as detailed by Vaastu-Shastra. In the modern world many top class magnetic instruments are there, and to find right direction, we should use these magnetic instruments, which are easy to use, and easily available also.

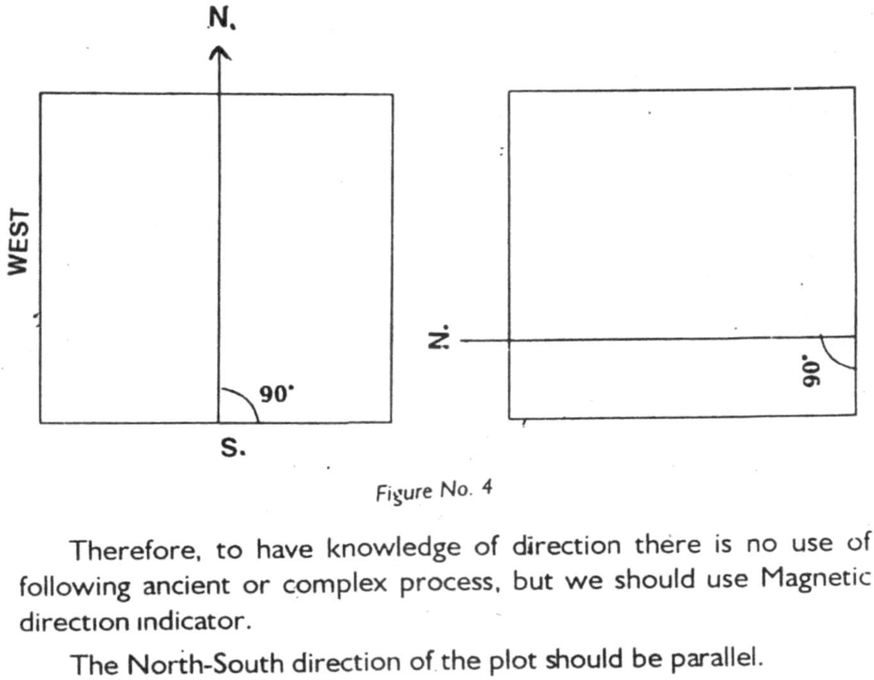

Figure No. 4

Therefore, to have knowledge of direction there is no use of following ancient or complex process, but we should use Magnetic direction indicator.

The North-South direction of the plot should be parallel.

In this way the position of the North and South of any plot should not have unequal angle or should not be dissimilar as shown in figure on next page.

If the plot is in the diverse angle, then one should leave that plot. If surrendering this angle plot is not possible then, before construction

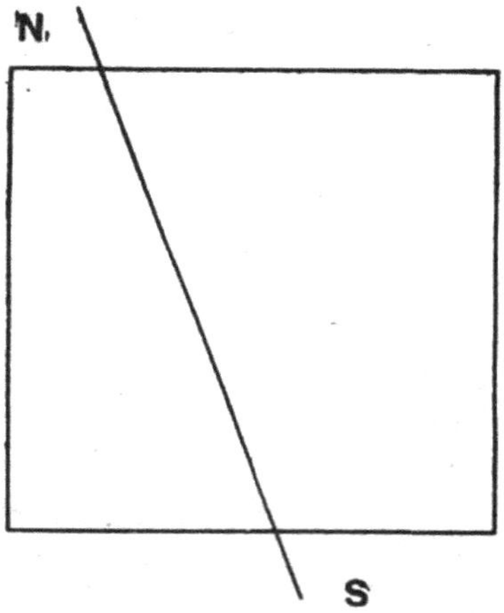

Figure No. 5

the plot should be purified and modified, as such type of plot is not suitable for construction of the house.

By the above said knowledge of direction we can find out direction position of the said plot very easily. If you retain in memory knowledge of your plot's direction; then only you can understand the Vaastu Shastra easily otherwise, the Vaastu Shastra is very complex to know and you can take wrong decision about the plot of your house. Until and unless you have right knowledge of direction, you won't have interest in this subject.

Types of Plots

Plots are gifted by the nature and man by his overt or covert urgings, has divided the plot into many forms & shapes. In this way the whole earth is divided into continents, countries, states, provinces, cities, colonies and lastly into small demarcated plots. This way we get the plots into many forms and shapes. Among these some plots are super best, some are medium and some plots are faulty as per vaastu-norms. Thus, while choosing the plot we should be very careful. In the Vishwakarma Prakash we have a beautiful couplet.

Chatursatram dwipakaram sidhekhhshreyabharupeneem!
Vrittapencha Bhadrapithanch trishulam lingasnibham!!
Prasadadhwaj kumbhadi dewanampi durlabham!
Trikornam shaktakarm shurbwyajansannibham!!
Murjakar sadresham sarpmnduk sapinim!
Kharajgar sankasham bakanchi pitrupinim!!
Mudgrabham tatholukak sarppmibham talha!
Shukrostaj sdrisham danuh parshurupinim!!
Krklasashwakaram durgabhyam vivarjaset!
Manorma chaya Bhumih parikhsheta prayatnath!!

(Viswakarma Prakash)

The plot that is squarely and whose shape is like elephant, lion, bull and horse, round shaped land with Trishul and Shivling and having aquarious in flag, such types of land are rare for Gods also.

Those plots which have Triangle-shape, ship or seed-shape,

having shapes of mridung, snake, frog, python, swan, bat, mallet, owl, pig, camel, goat, bow, dead body, spade are plots not to be taken in the view of vaastu.

The rectangular, circular and square plots are the best plots. People residing in the rectangular plots are prosperous. Most of their complex works are solved very easily. People residing in the square plots have no problem of money. They have money from different forms. People living on the circular plots have intelligence and brain. They handle their jobs very easily by their wisdom. The people who reside in Bhadrapeeth plot have very mild nature. They are always eagar to help everyone. God also helps those men.

The holymen and our ancient teachers have said, about the land, that our eyes analyse the land first of all 'Eye sight should be very alert and is mentally gifted. Eyesight is related to intellect. Thus by seeing the plot, if it suits our eyesight, then that land is said to be best to some extent, and we should reside there.

If the plot have creepers, medicinal & healthy plants, Neem and Asiatic Greevia, sweet soil, soft earth, pure air then the people or the landlord have all the comforts of heaven as the travellers will come there and have rest and will feel happy and contented.

As the food which is upto our satisfaction makes our body feel happy and healthy from inside, just like that the plot, giving happiness to our mind gives calm feeling to our whole body.

Therefore the conclusion is that all types of Lands are not suitable for residing. In vaastu shastra, first of all soil is analysed and thereafter plot is selected.

Best quality of plots are as following—

Square Right Angled plot

Square, Equal angled, quadriangled plot is of best quality, according to the Vaastu Shastra. People residing in this plot get mental and financial peace.

Rectangular Right Angled plot.

This type of plot is said to be the best plot. In the rectangular, plot one should keep in mind that its length & breadlth should not be more than 1:2. The people living in these plots are happy and prosperous.

Square Right Angled plot

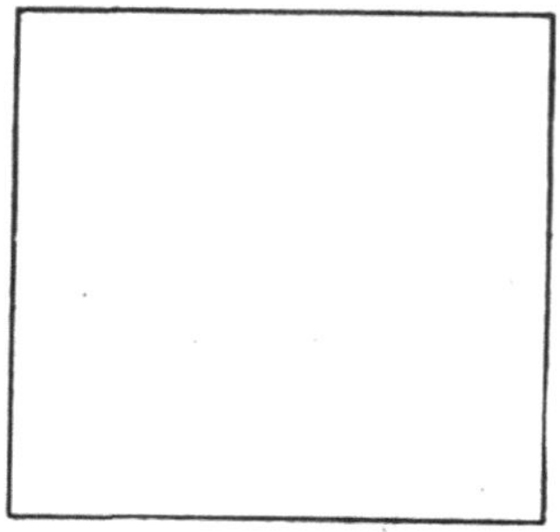

Rectangular Right Angled plot

Circular plot

Circular plot is of 360° angled. In vaastu shastra these types of plots are of very superior quality and are very rare to find. The whole family of the Landlords are always happy and prosperous.

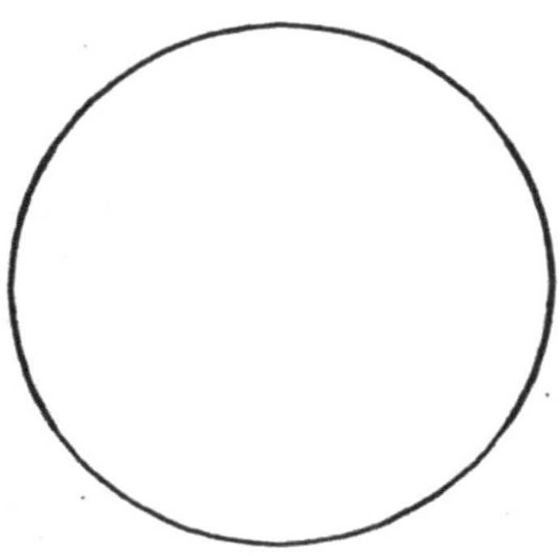

Different Types of Land

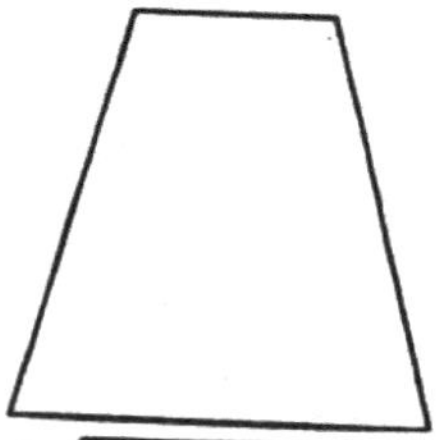

***Quadriangled trapezium plot*—**
This plot is not good, people residing here are always victim of illusion.

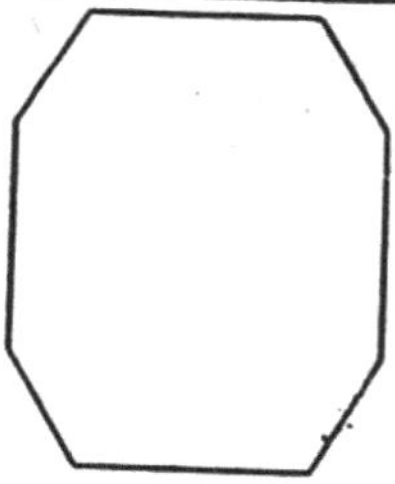

***Eight angled Long plot*—**
This plot gives pain suffering and trouble. People residing in this plot have many types of troubles and they have long troubles with doctors and advocates.

***Two angled arched Plot*—**
This plot is said to add to lots of enemies.

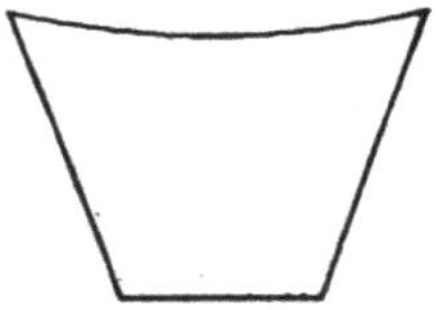

***Bucket shaped plot*—**
The people residing in this plot are always neck-deep in debt.

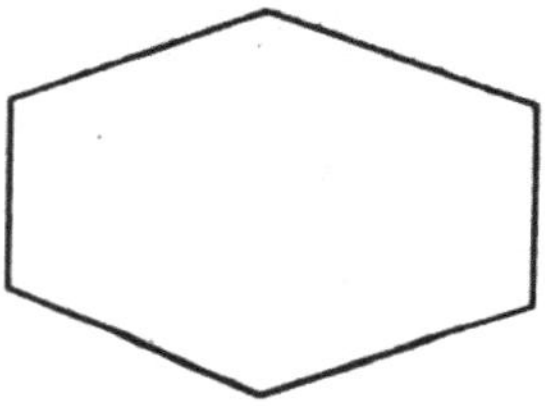

***Mridung(drum) shaped plot*—**
The Landlord residing in this plot infatuates towards other lady and the Landlord wastes away too much money.

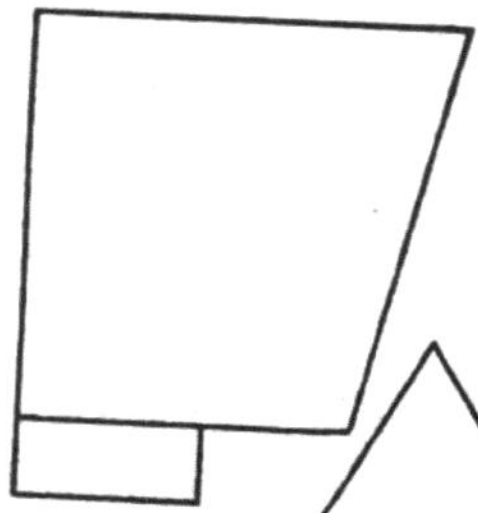

Crow's Beak-shaped plot—

This plot is said to be of best category. The people who reside here become very rich and prosperous.

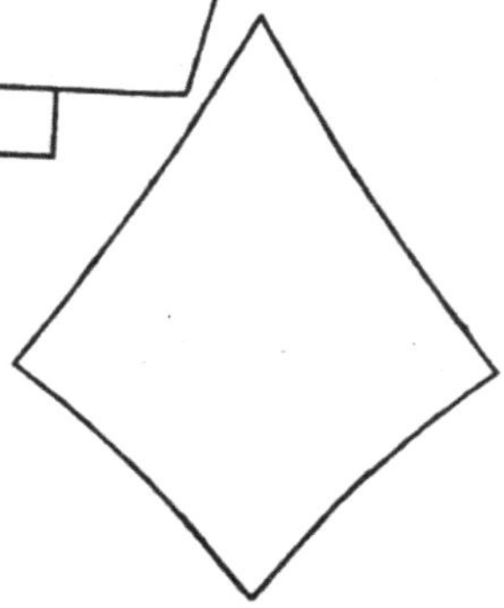

Diamond shaped plot—

This plot is said not to be good. There is always dispute between the husband and the wife living on this plot.

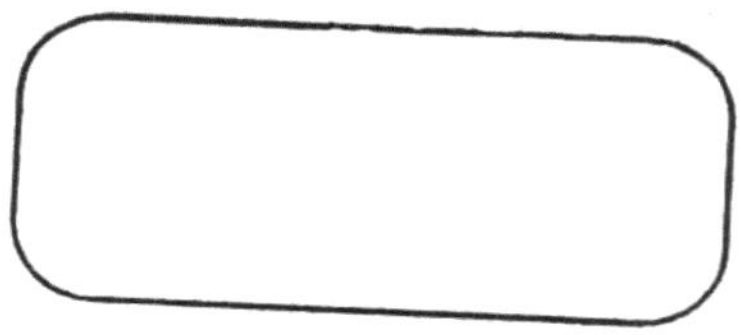

Capsule like plot—

This plot is of mixed nature. The people living here are always sad and indifferent.

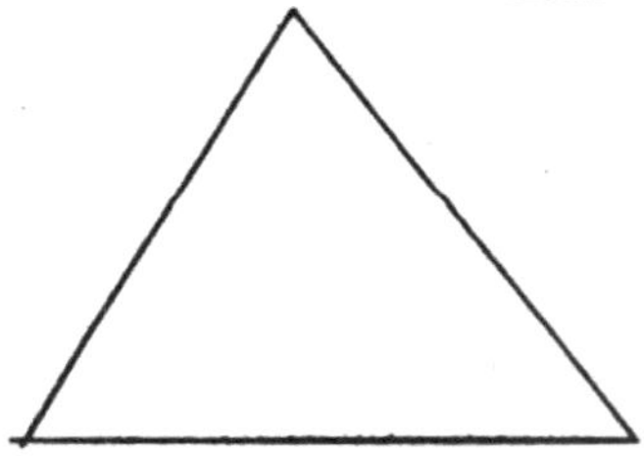

Triangle like plot—

This is said to be ill-omened. The people who live here can never accumulate money.

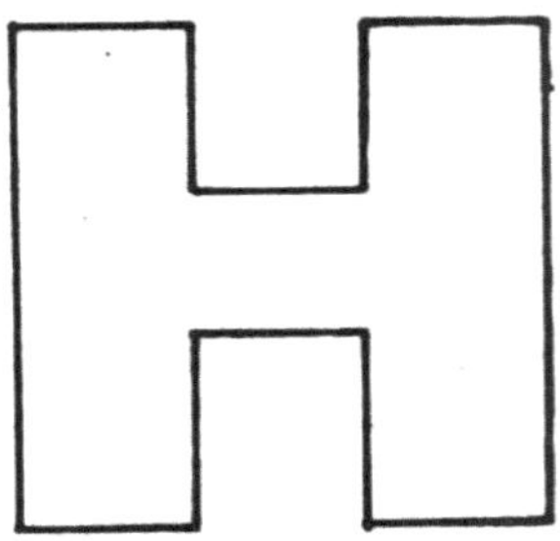

H - Shaped plot—

Such a plot is never seen by me. Some Vaastu Shastri had mentioned about this plot. This plot is not good.

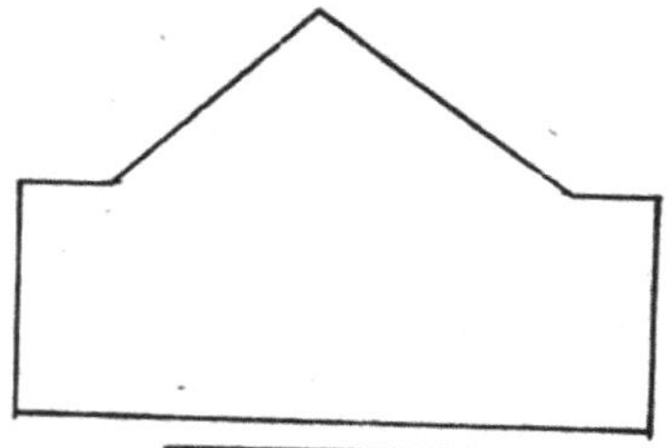

Temple like plot—

This plot is said to be free from any problem or tension. The people who reside here are seen to be carefree and they renouce their houses after worldly detachment.

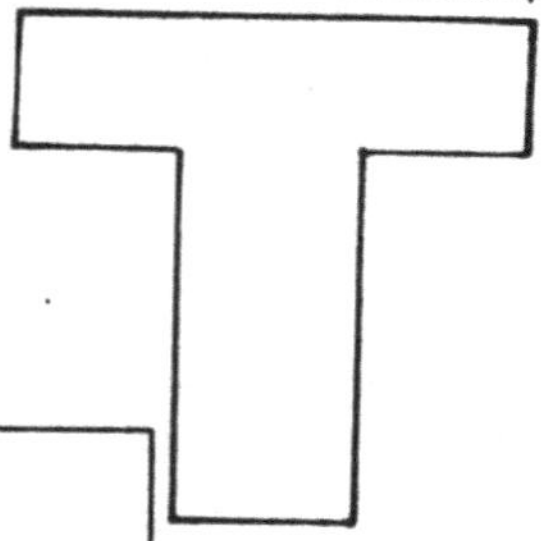

T — Shaped plot—

I have seen people selling their houses within four-five years, who live in this type of plots. The fifth buyer of this plot is said to be cheerful upto some limit.

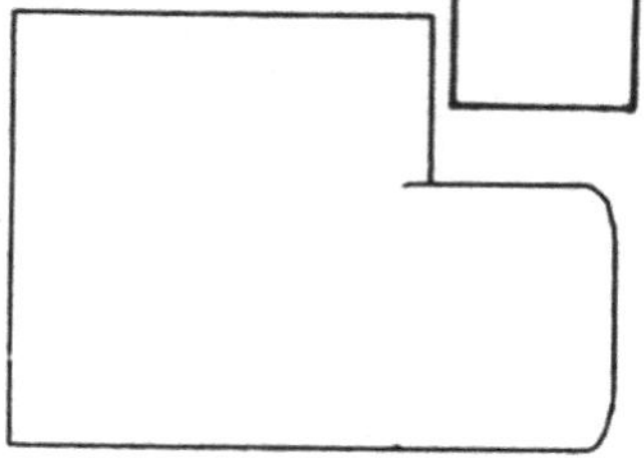

Wing like plot—

This is the worst plot. The money is ruined here. The people who live here become beggars.

Half moon like plot—

This type of plots are seen only in the books, leaving aside rare exception.

The plots, which have been seen in the above diagrams, are very difficult to be found in this modern world. The people who buy the plots to build their houses want square plots, because square plots are liked by all people, and also they are easy to dispose of.

Therefore, while demarcating land into different plots, it is very essential to keep in mind that no plot should be of peculiar shape. The square plots are sold very easily. The plots which are of peculiar or unusual shapes are not sold easily, and it is very difficult to remodel the plot according to the desirable shape. These types of plots, are better not opted for

Plots on different roads.

Many types of direction faced plots are found due to different roads and directions. Due to change in direction and roads the results of the plots falls differently on the landlord. Besides these, the qualities of these plots depend upon the direction and the roads.

Different plots on one road.

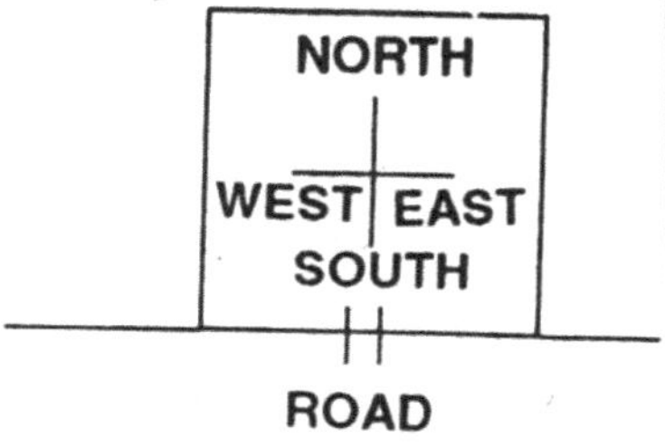

South-faced plot on one side of the road— South is to the door of God of death. Therefore donot buy this type of plot as far as possible.

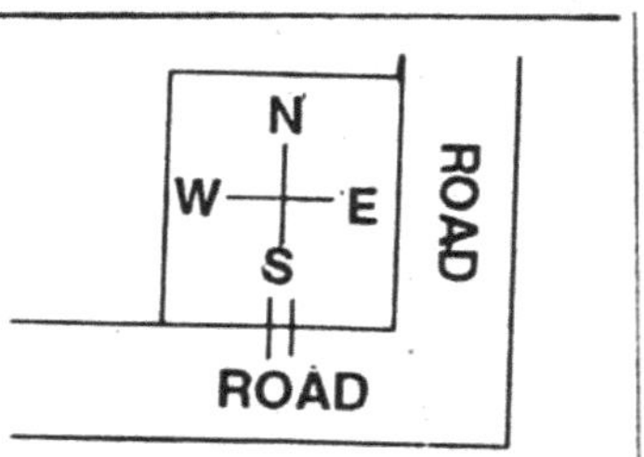

South-faced plot with passage on the two sides— This plot is of good category. The person living here has become famous doctor. This plot is good for the businessman. Here there is only one road.

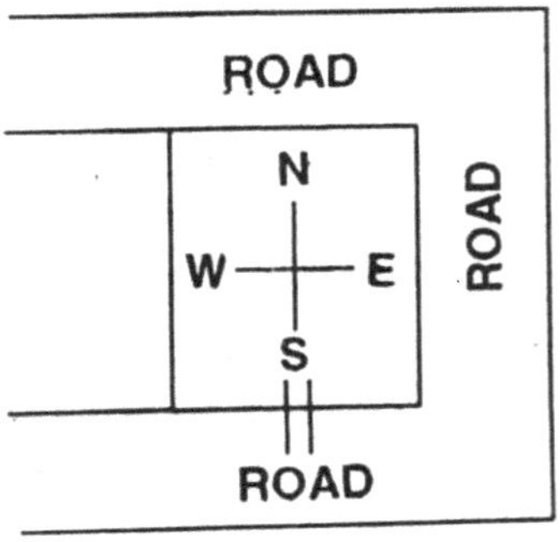

South-faced plot with passage on the three sides— This plot is said to be the best for the Iron traders. The new generation gets very prosperous on this plot.

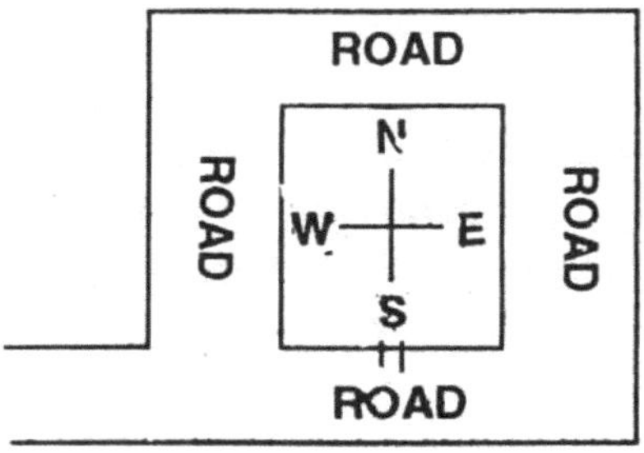

South-faced plot with passage on the four sides— This plot is best for the panshop. Beside this, the plot is also good for T.V. and Radio traders. There is only one way here.

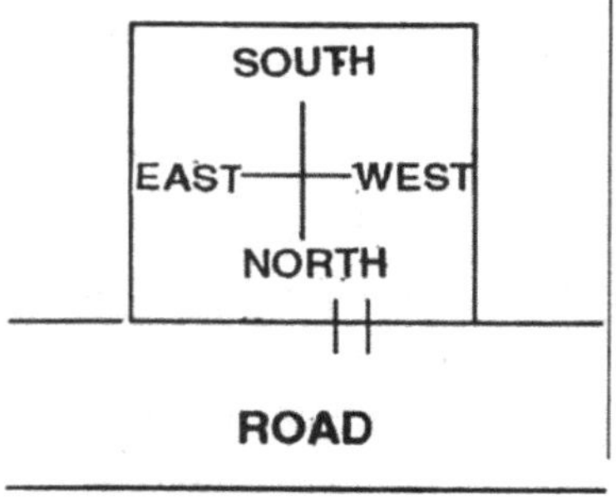

North-faced plot on one side of the road— This plot is good for the family people. The middle class people are very happy here.

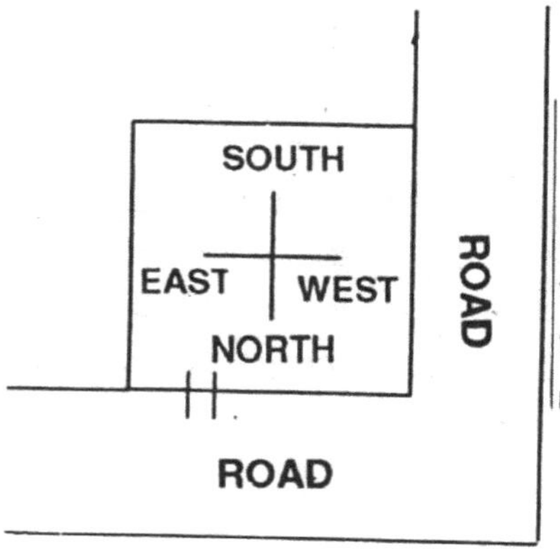

North-faced plot with passage on the two sides— This plot is best for the family people. The people residing here will live very peacefully.

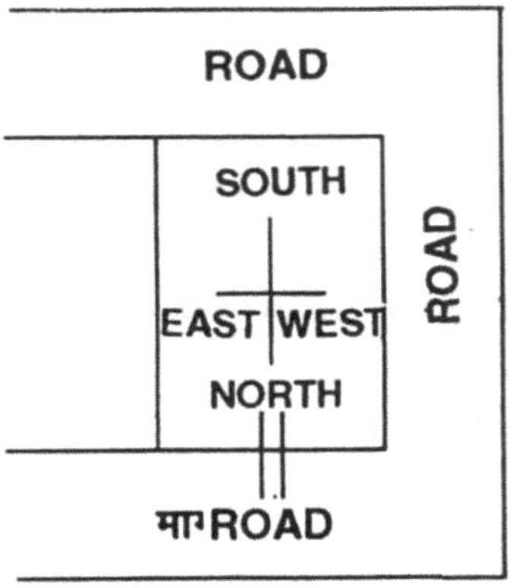

North-faced plot with passage on the three sides— This plot is said to be the best for the business. For Picture hall hotel and restaurant this plot gives good results. Here there is only one pathway.

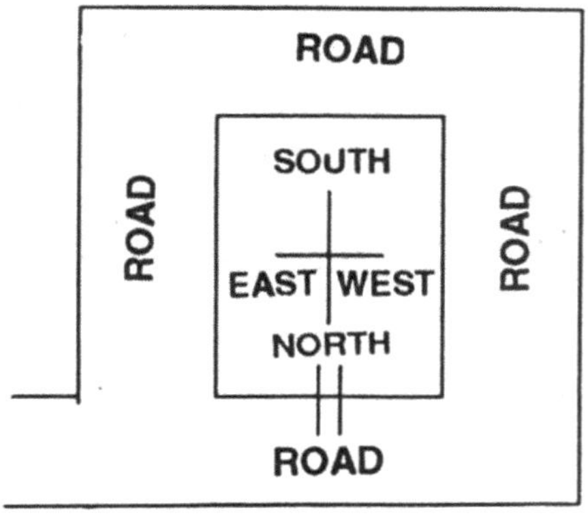

North-faced plot with passage on the four sides— This plot is of best category. This is profitable both for the family people and the businessman. The people residing on this plot get profit from all avenues. There is only one way here.

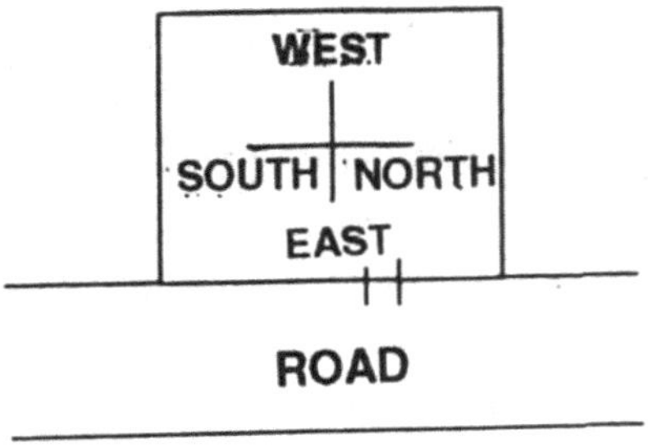

East-faced plot on one side of the road— This plot is said to be of best quality. The people residing on this plot remain healthy throughout their life. There is only one way here.

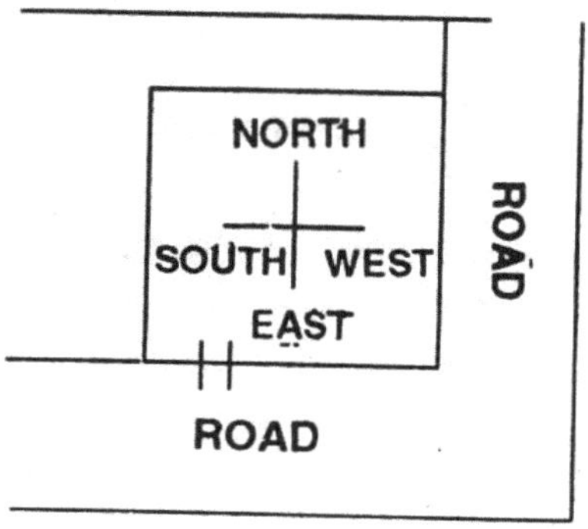

East-faced plot with passage on the two sides— This plot is best for family and also for medicine shop. There is only one way here.

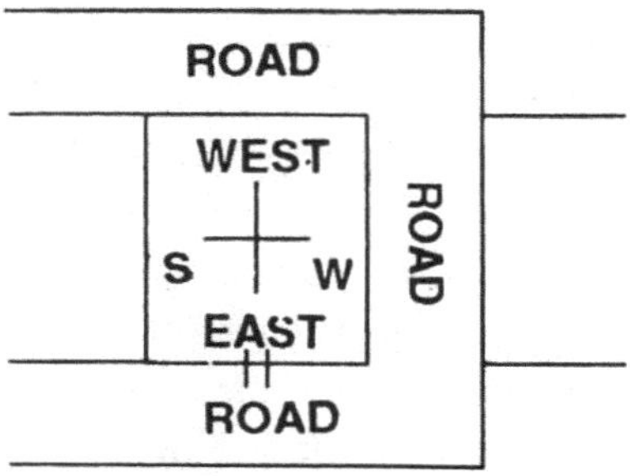

East-faced plot with passage on the three sides— This plot is best for family, cinema hall, hotel, nursing home and school. The lord Indra lives here.

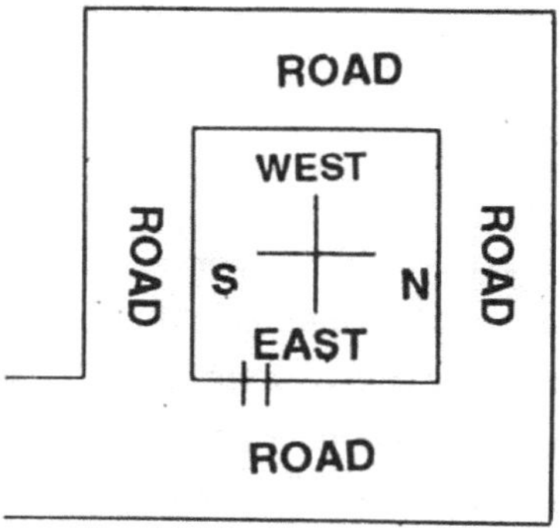

East-faced plot with passage on the four sides— This plot is best for the big business. Among the East-facing plots this plot is unique. I have myself seen only one or two of this type of plots. This plot is very valuable and is very rare to find.

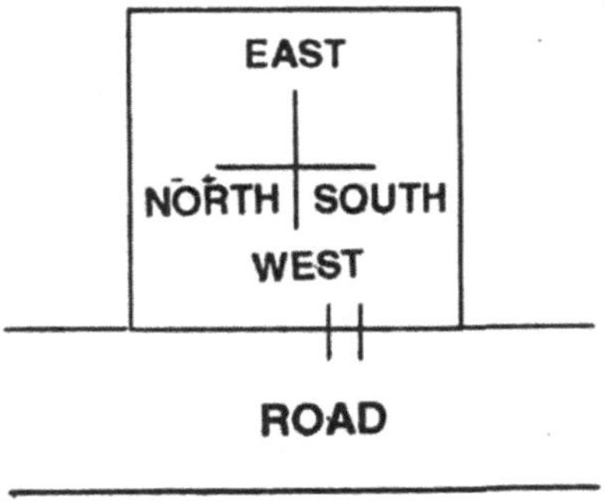

West-faced plot on one side of the road— This plot is good for the family life.

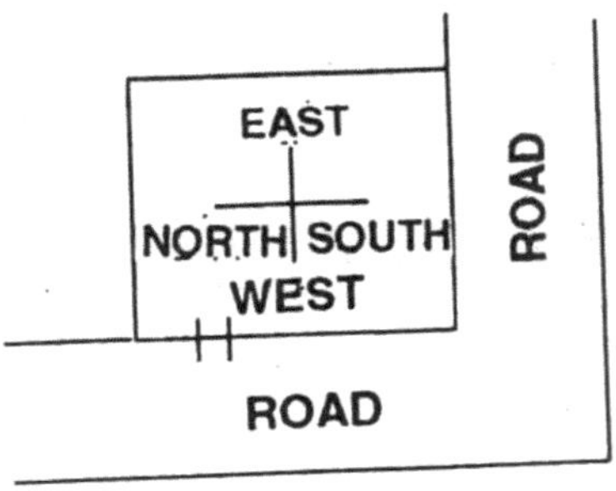

West-faced plot with passage on the two sides— This plot is considered in the best category. This plot is equally good for businessman and familyman.

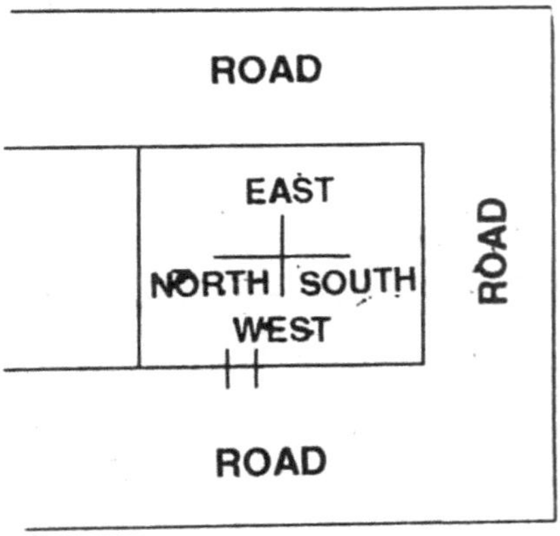

West-faced plot with passage on the three sides— This plot is best for the business, as it is very profitable. There is only one way here.

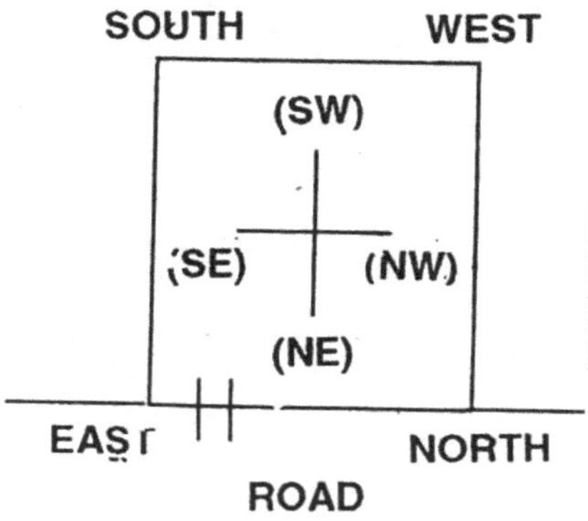

Ishan or North-East faced plot on one side of road— This plot is not good from the entrance point of view. Ishan is said to be the place of worship. Therefore, Ishan plot with one road is not good.

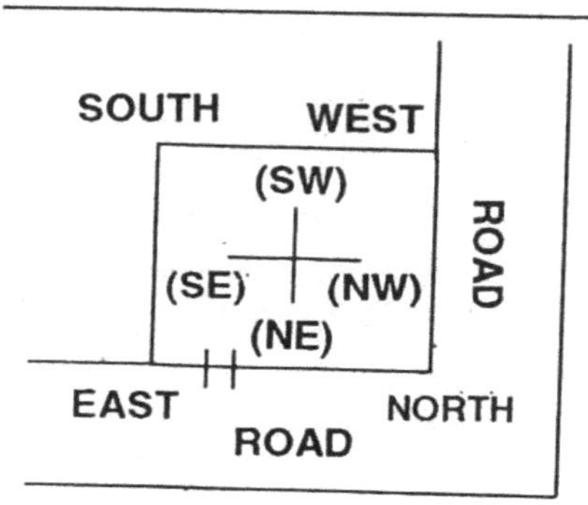

Ishan or North-East-faced plot with passage on the two sides— This is an ordinary type of plot, which will give common result to the family living there. There is only one way here.

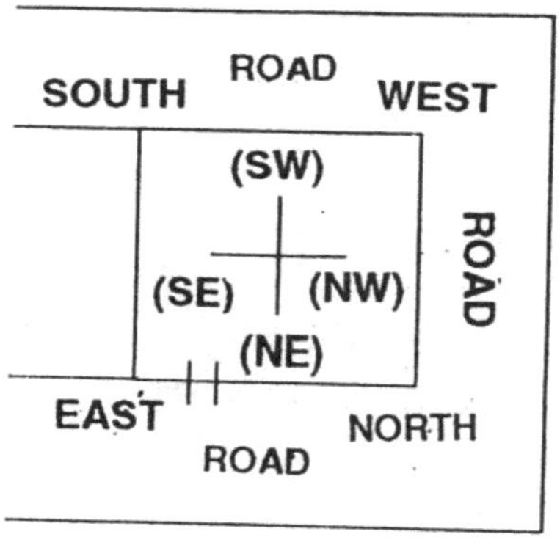

Ishan or North East faced plot with passage on the three sides— This plot is good for family, business and small industries.

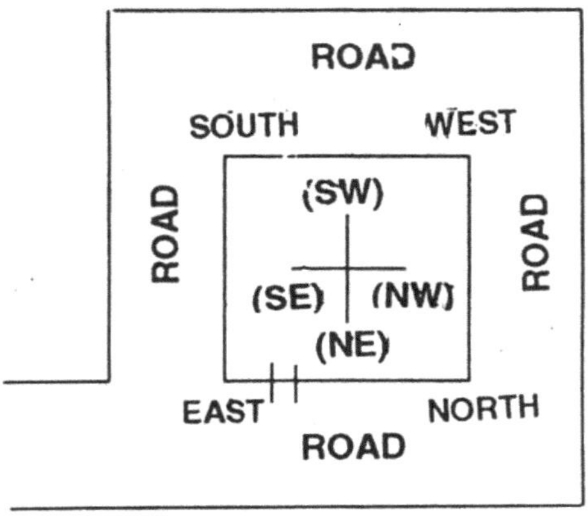

Ishan or North East faced plot with passage on the four sides— This is best for the businessman. There is only one way here.

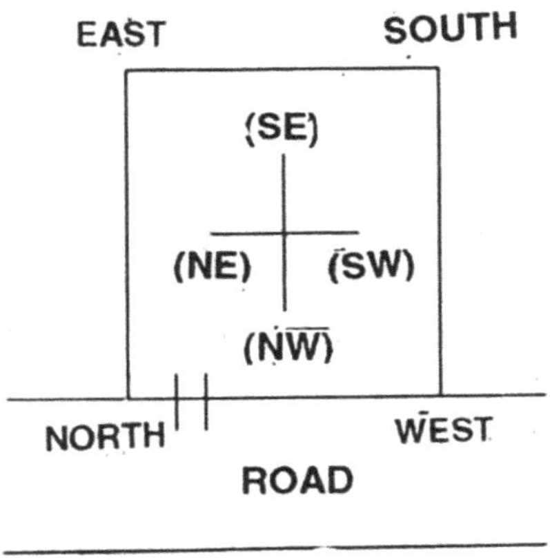

Wayava or North-West-faced plot on one side of the road— This is not a good plot. This plot gives unhappiness and unrest. There is only one way here.

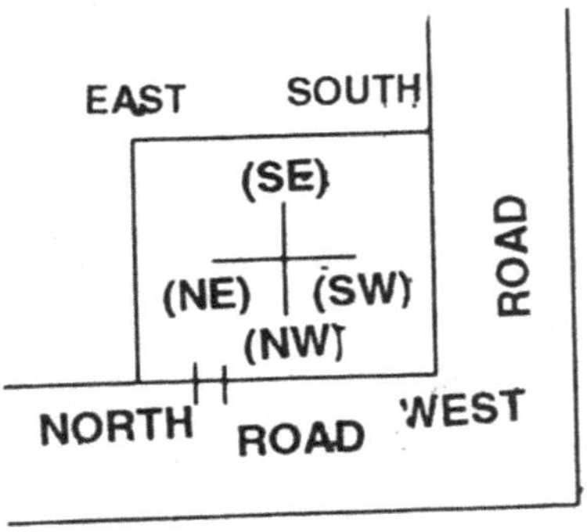

Wayava or North West faced plot with passage on the two sides— This plot is of good quality and here is only one way.

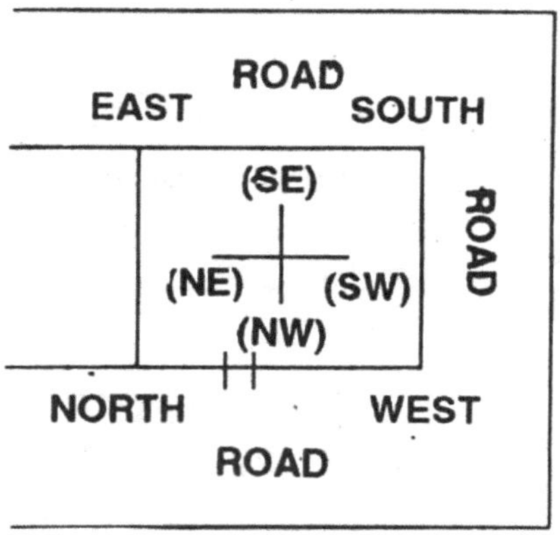

Wayava or North-West-faced plot with passage on the three sides— This plot is of ordinary type. The people residing here has to travel too much. There is only one way here.

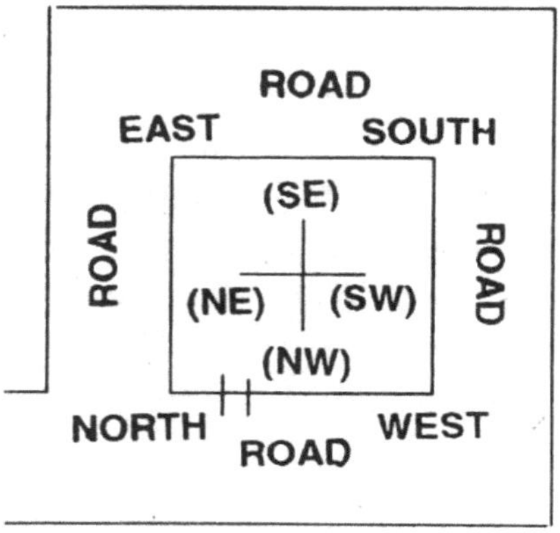

Wayava or North-West-faced plot with passage on the four sides— This plot is not of good type. This plot is good only for cottage or resorts. There is only one way.

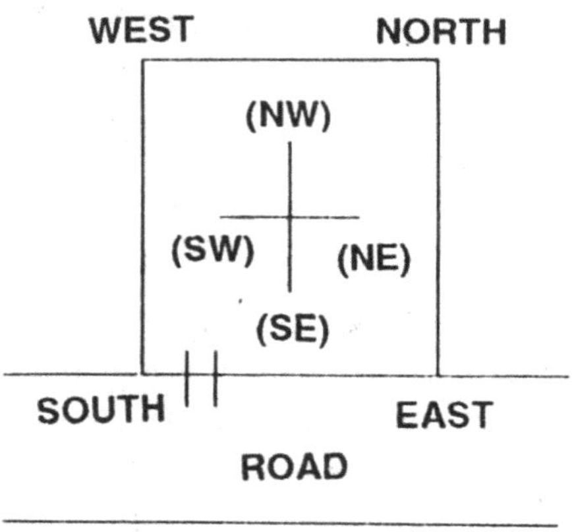

Agnaya or South-East-faced plot on one side of the road— This plot is profitable for Iron foundry, lime factory, colour factory, hot machines welding, hotel etc.

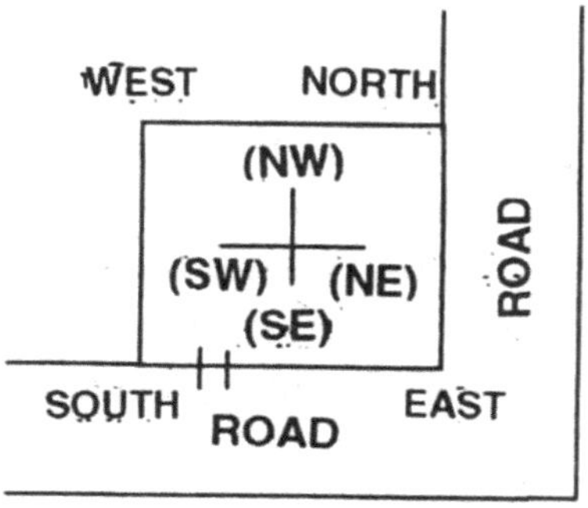

Agnaya or South East faced plot with passage on the two sides— This is best for Iron foundry and machinery. This plot is not suitable for family. There is only one way here.

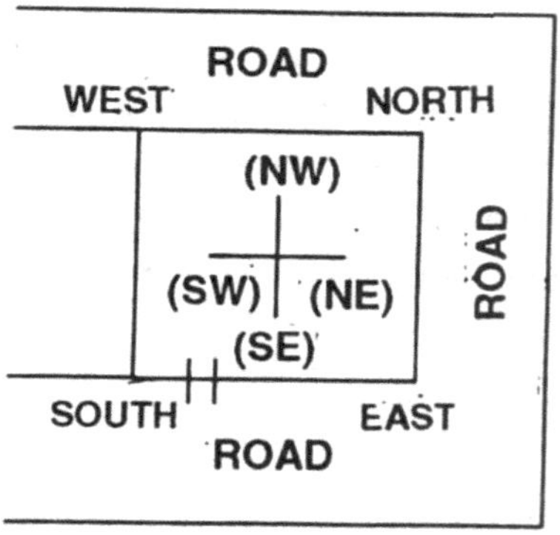

Agnaya or South East faced plot with passage on the three sides— This plot is good for businessman and is best for bar owners. Bar on this plot will fetch a lot of money to the owner. For bar there is no plot better than this. There is only way here.

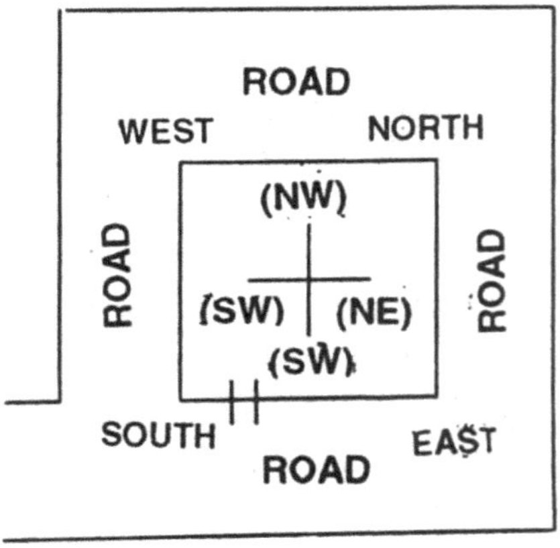

Agnaya or South-East-faced plot with passage on the four sides— This plot is best for the electricity foundation. T.V. factory, Telephone Bhawan or for big factories. Family should not live here because theft will be there, servant will always go away. There is only one way here.

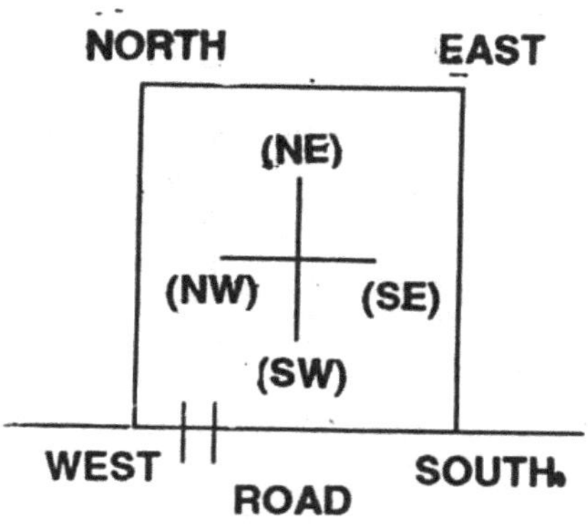

Nairithaya or South-West-faced plot on one side of the road— This plot is not good. People residing here always feel a peculiar and bad smell which means there is something which is akin to some dead animal's foul smell. This plot gives sadness.

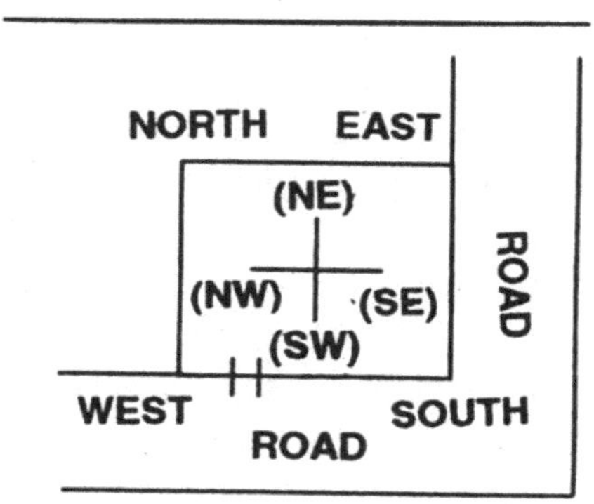

Nairithaya or South-West-faced plot with passage on the two sides— This plot is of ordinary type. It is good for business but not fruitful for family. There is only one way.

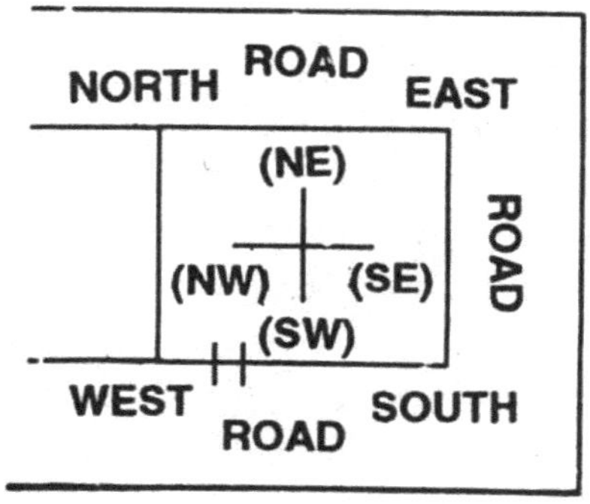

Nairithaya or South-West-faced plot with passage on the three sides— This plot is very good for the business- men. There will be good sale of apparatus related to the doctor's operation. If there is a nursing home here, the plot-owner will become very rich. There is no plot better than this plot for running a nursing home. There is only one way.

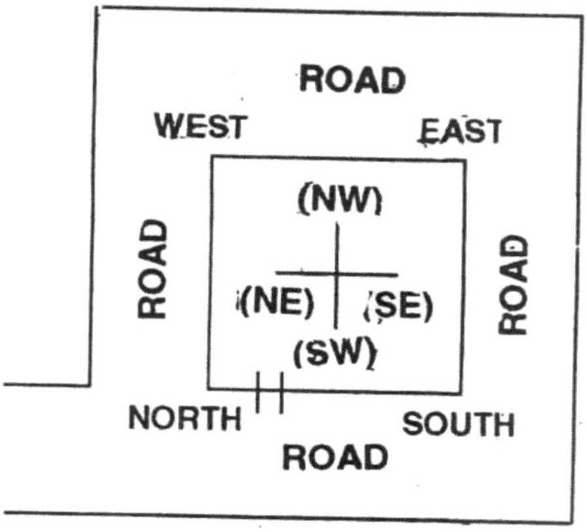

Nairithaya or South-West-faced plot with passage on the four sides— This plot is best for the first generation. The second generation should not live here. If they stay here, they will be destroyed in the litigation. They can even get mad. There is only one way here.

Till now we have studied about the plots which are situated with one road only. Among them, some are not found. And, if it is found in negligible numbers yet from the point of study of vaastu it is neccessary to discuss it.

In the same way, we can find different types of plots on intersection of different roads, in different directions.

Two roads on the two sides of the plot

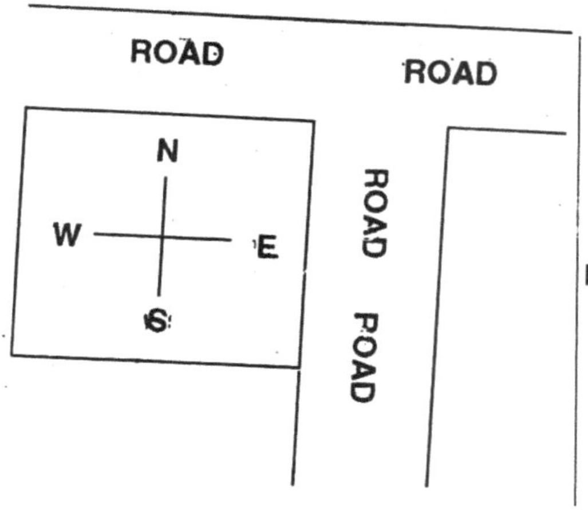

Best plot & will give wealth.

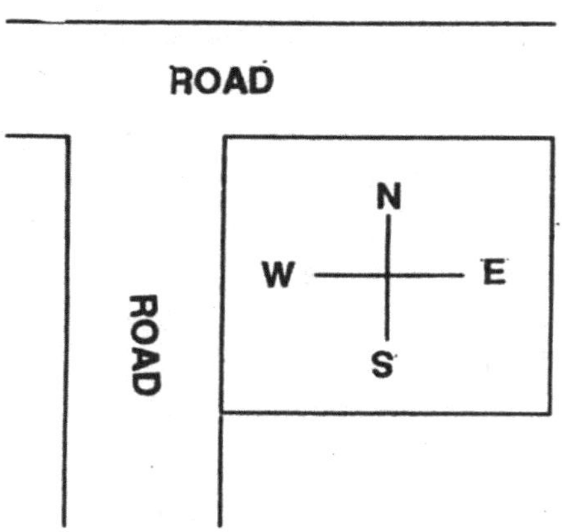

Best plot & will augur well for progeny

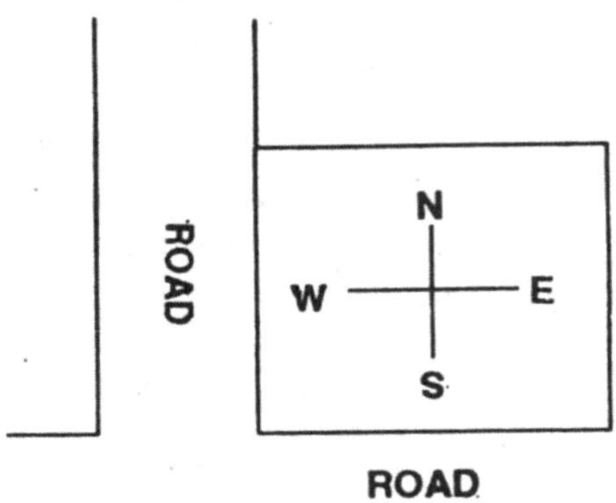

Peaceful & ordinary plot.

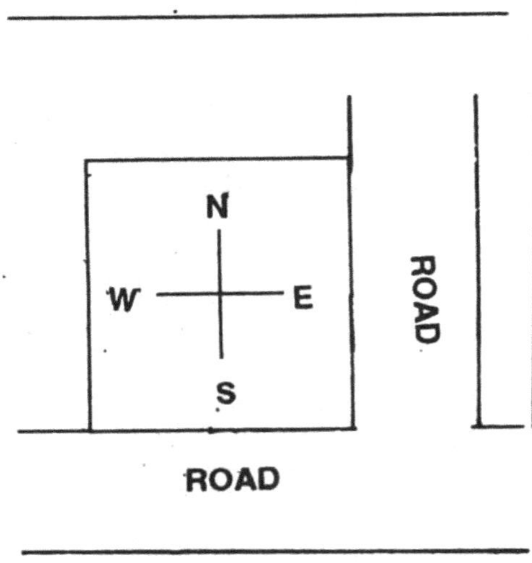

It is an inferior and ignorable plot.

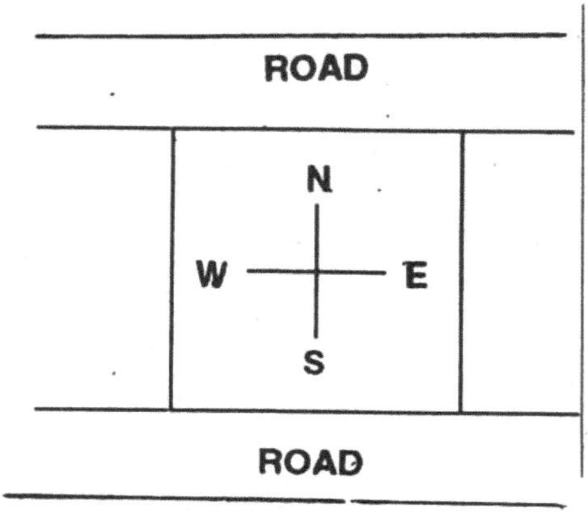

Best plot

Plot is suitable for the middle class family.

Three roads on the three sides of the plot

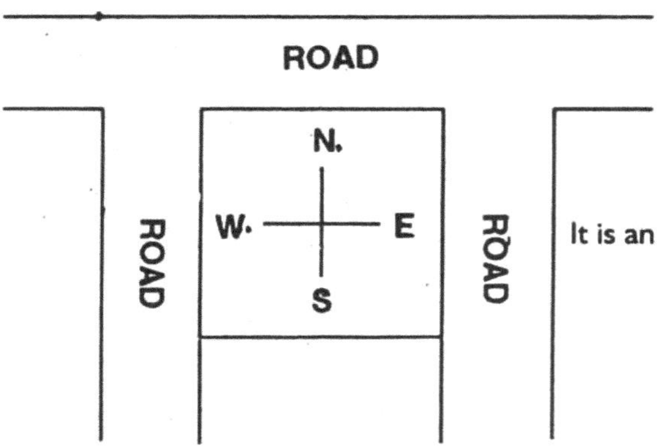

It is an inauspicious plot.

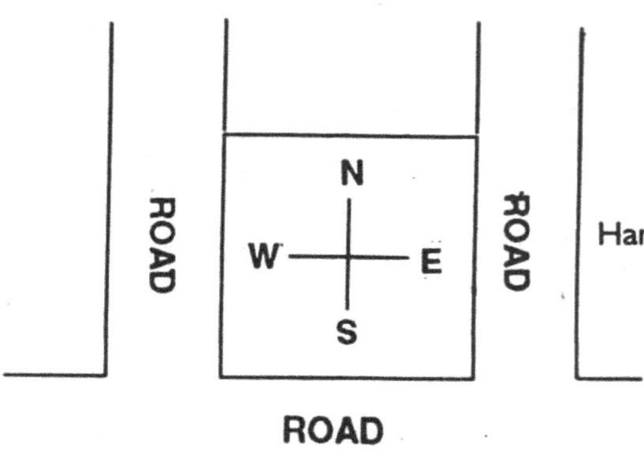

Harmful plot.

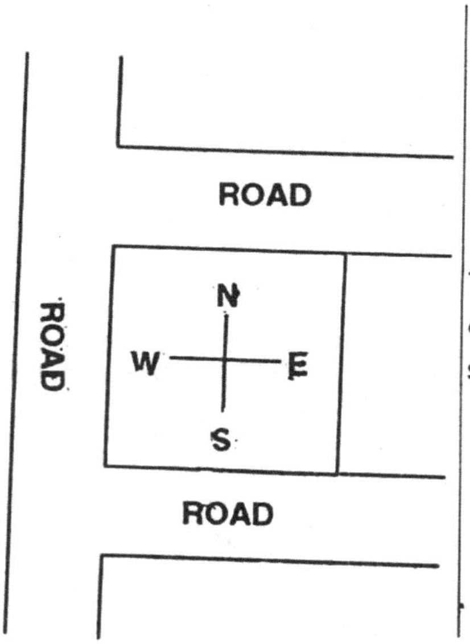

This plot will always prove ominous for the owner. This plot should be abandoned.

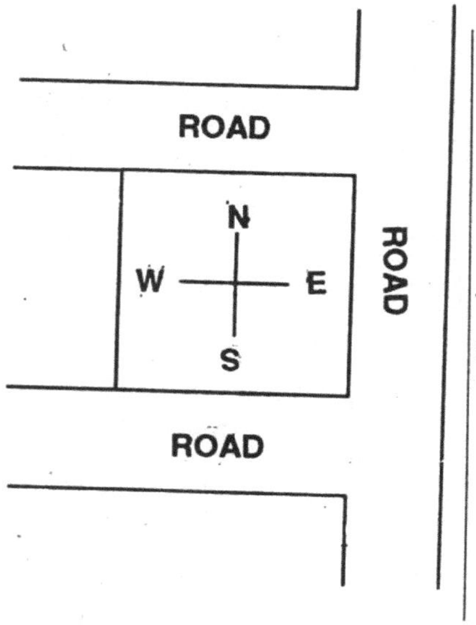

This plot is good for low and middle class families.

Four roads on the four sides of the plot

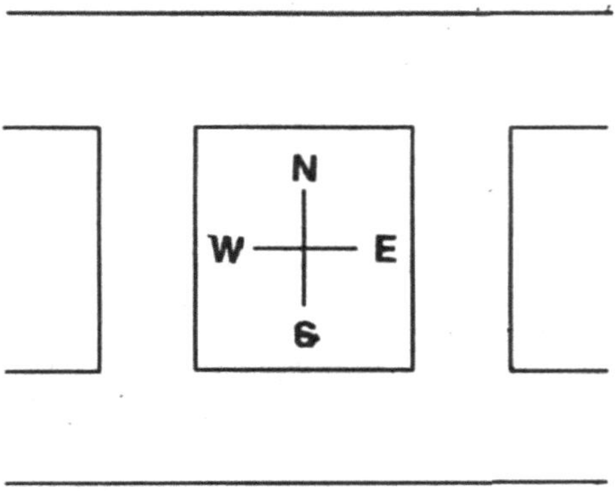

This plot having four roads is the best plot. The people residing here will never get poor.

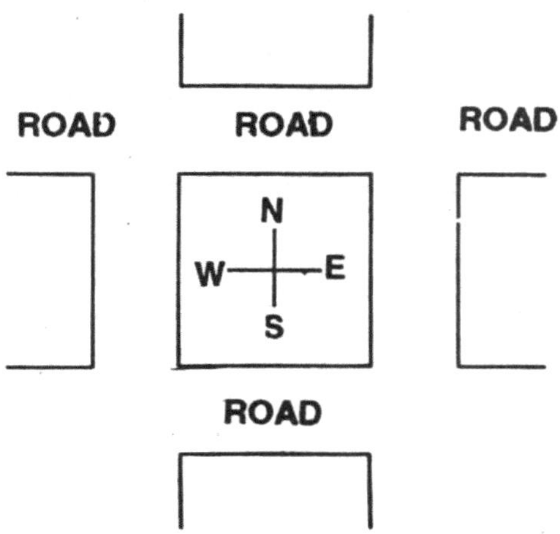

A plot situated between the four crossings of roads is found only one or two in a town. This unique plot is good for making multistoryed buildings.

Land with vedh fault

There are many types of faults found, but the path-fault found on the plots are called Path-vedh fault. Path-vedh fault depends upon the joints and direction of the path ways. Land vedh can occur due to temple, trees, mud, pole, wire, drain or flags, however we shall consider only those vedhs which are created out of road/path joints we have to think here of only the vedh of path joint.

If there is path vedh on any plot, then it is better to abandon it because ultimately fault is a fault. Some Vaastu Shastri had said that Ishan or North- East-faced plot has no vedh-fault but, as far as I have seen, path-vedh fault on any type of plot gives diseases to the family members and for businessmen it is not good for their economic aspect.

Clear diagrams to show path vedh, follow on subsequent pages.

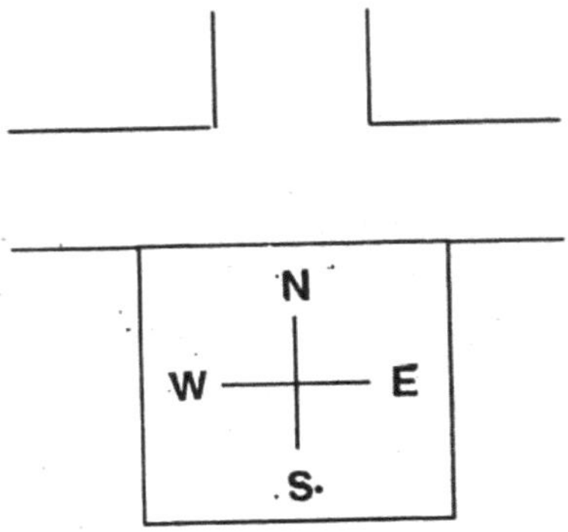

If the North faced plot has vedh fault in the Ishan or North-East face or angle, then the fault is ordinary fault. You should leave open this side of Ishan. Thus the fault will go away and the rest of the land of the plot can be used.

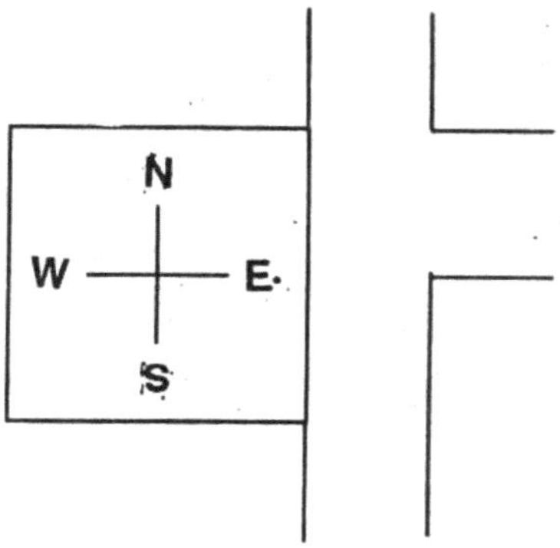

If the East faced plot has vedh fault in the Ishan side, then the fault is within the normal fault. You should leave this side and make the house on the rest of the plot. This fault is not much harmful.

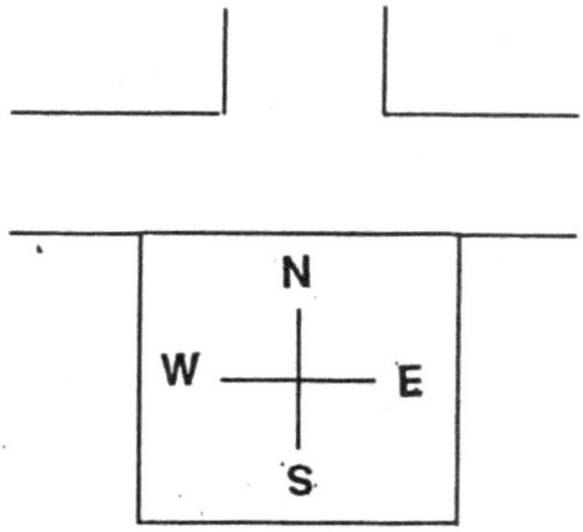

If North-faced plot has the vedh fault at the middle of the plot, then the plot is highly harmful. This plot should be abandoned, as it may be a cause for divorce and some dispute..

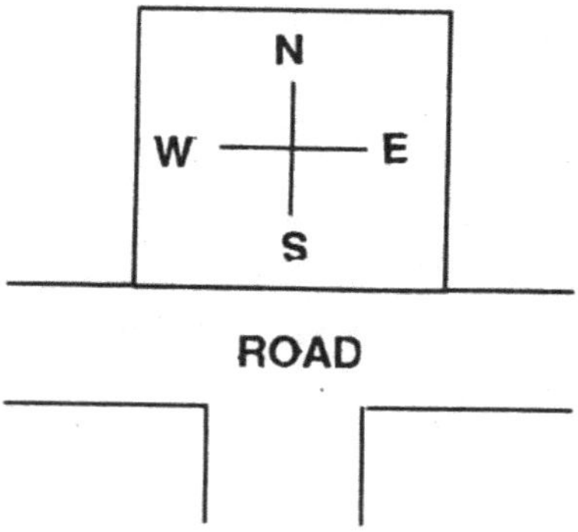

South-faced plot having vedh-fault at the middle of the plot, then the plot is said to be faulty. This plot should be rejected. The people residing here will be economically poor.

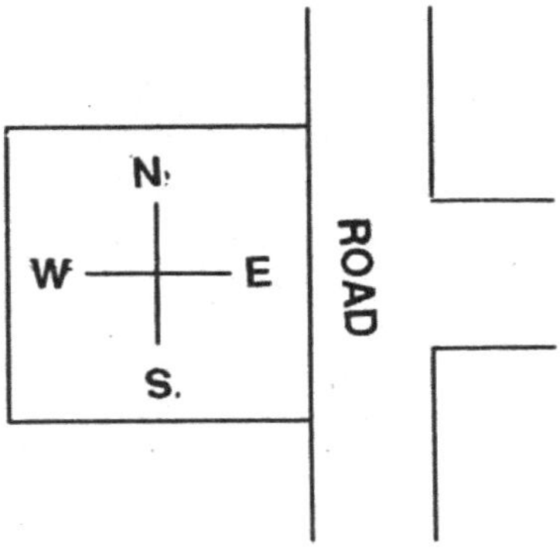

If the East-faced plot has vedh at the middle of the plot then the plot is harmful. I have seen people getting sick very badly who reside here. The wealth of the family disappears before the marriage of the daughter. This plot should be abandoned.

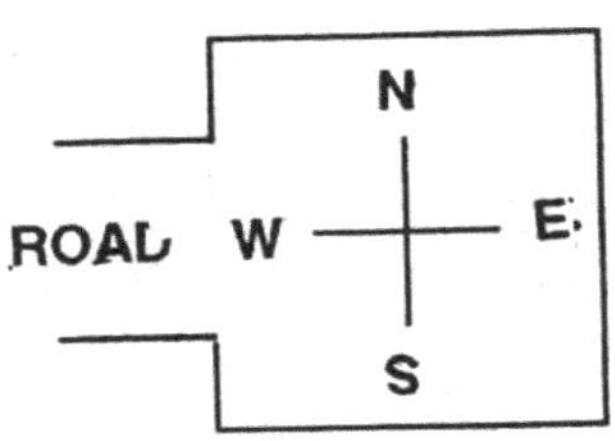

If the West faced plot has vedh fault at middle of the plot, then the plot should be better left. This path vedh-affects mentally.

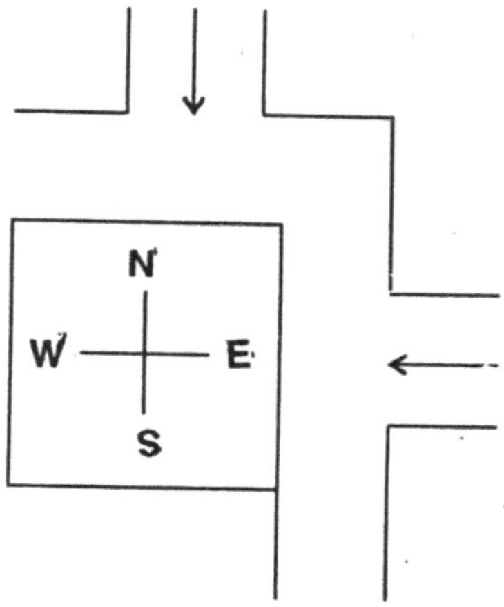

If the East faced plot has path vedh fault in East & North direction, then the plot should be rejected. There is abundant quantity of poisonous snakes & reptiles in such land. Therefore, there is always fear of death by poison or snake-biting. If there is an Iron factory on this plot then the Iron disappears in the soil, and it will often remain closed.

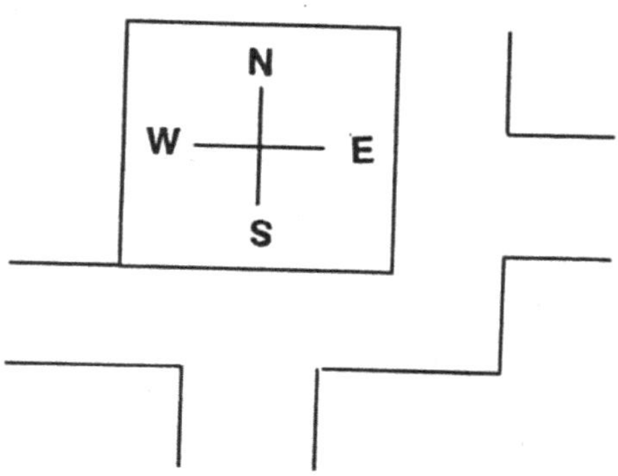

If the East faced plot has vedh-fault in East & South direction, then the plot should be rejected. This plot is death prone. This plot makes the people bankrupt who are residing here.

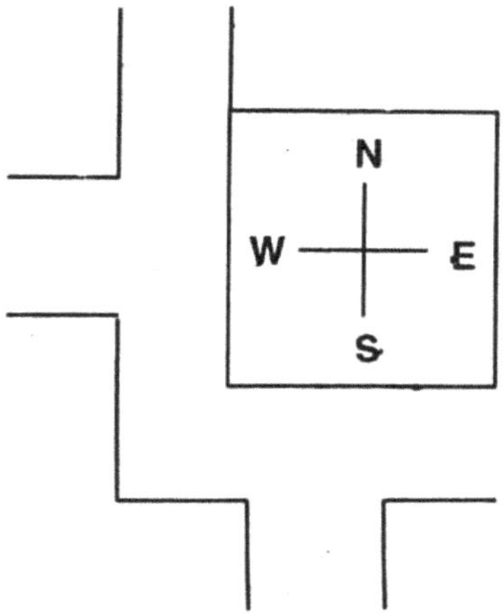

If the South faced plot has path-vedh fault in South & North direction then the plot should be better left.

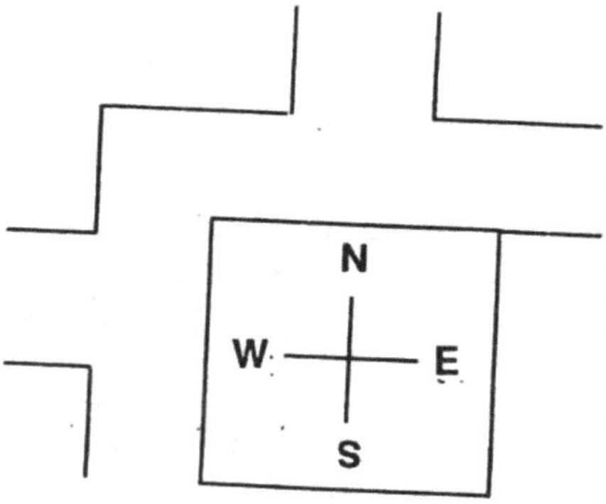

If the North faced plot has vedh-fault in North & West direction, then the plot should be rejected. The people who reside here face extravagance and get defame. Entire fame of the landlord turns into defamation.

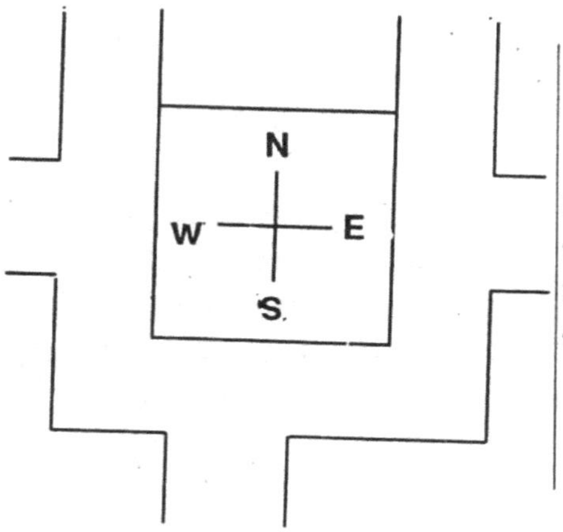

If the plot has East, West & South vedh-fault, then the plot is harmful, but the plot can be used by an iron trader.

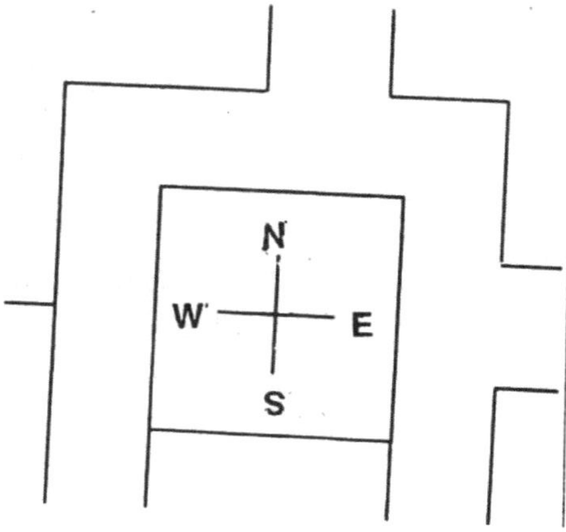

If the West faced plot has vedh fault in West, East & North direction then the plot is harmful. This plot can be used for the stock of cement. It is good for holiday resort also.

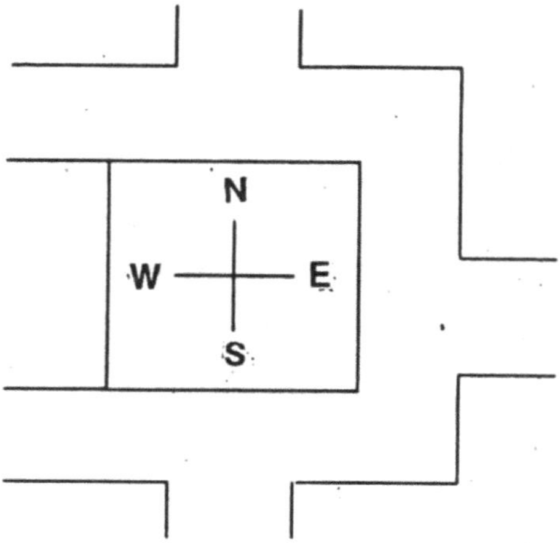

If the South faced plot has vedh fault in North & East then the plot should be rejected. The furniture buisness showroom will prosper in this plot. I have seen a prosperous furniture showroom on this type of plot. The owner of this showroom has bought more shops through earning from this one shop & has become a richman.

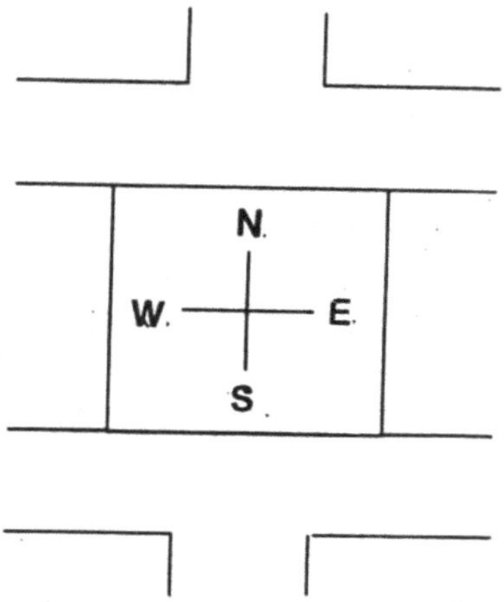

If a plot has vedh fault in the middle of two directions & it is in the South & North direction then the plot is harmful. The landlord of this plot faces many types of troubles & problems. Therefore this land should be better left.

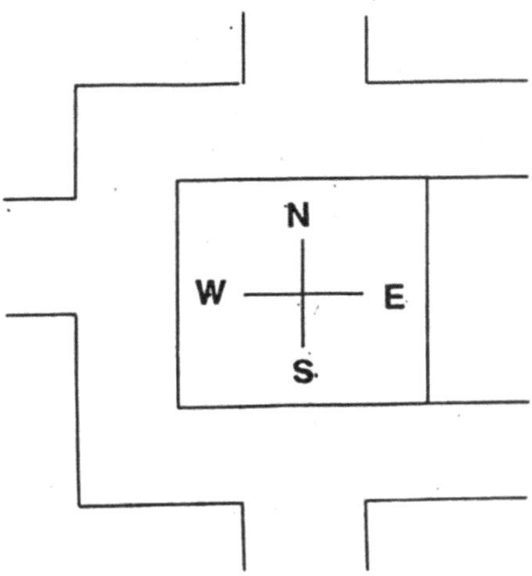

If the West faced plot has vedh fault in North, West & South direction then the plot should be left outrightly. The people residing on this plot face many suspicious problems.

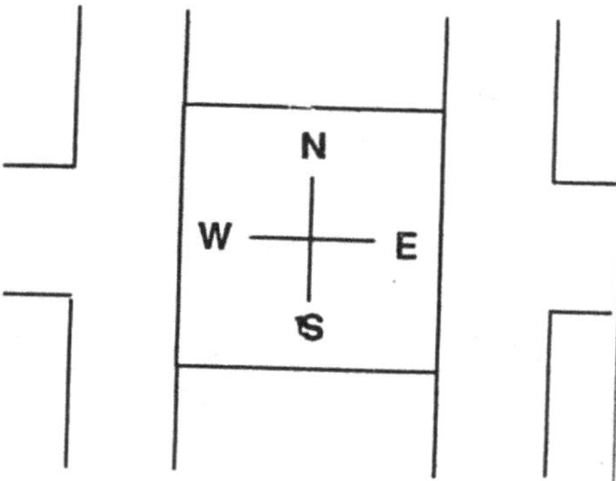

If a plot has vedh fault in East & West direction then the plot is harmful. The people who live there will not be comfortable, the husband-wife relationship will break. Their children will stay far away.

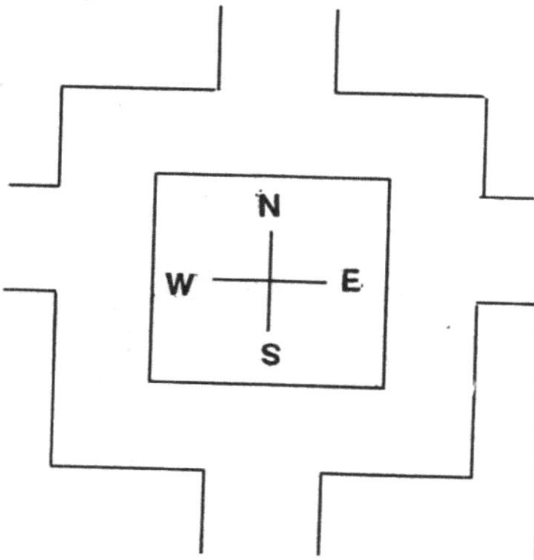

If a plot has path vedh fault in all the four directions then the plot is very harmful & faulty. The people residing on this plot will suffer from severe accidents, with major injuries operations, stiches on the face etc.This plot should be left.

The plots which we have discussed above with various path-vedhas are rarely found. People who buy a large piece of land and cut plots out of it do not take the risk of making such plots useless. Suppose if you ever find such a kind of plot you should never buy it. In order to attain knowledge of Vaastu I have given detailed description of all the drawbacks.

Last Plot on Closed Road

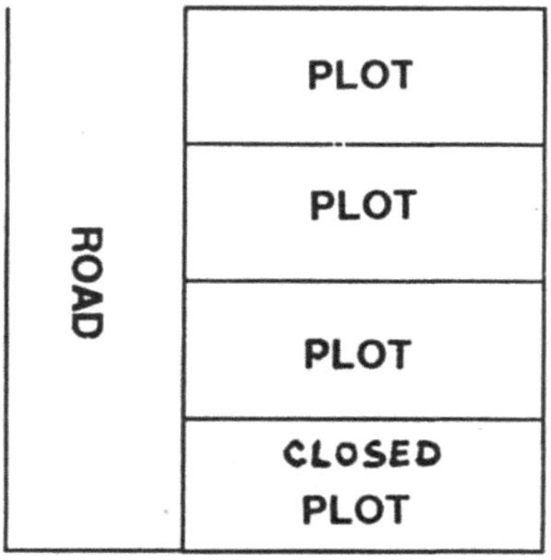

Such kind of plots are generally found in colonies because there are several houses in colonies. So, such kind of plot is eventually formed in the residential areas but in vaastushastra such kind of corner plots are considered to be unsuitable. It could be harmful for both residence and business purposes. Hence closed-corner plot should not be bought.

Mandir vedh (Temple Obstacle) : Existence of a temple or any holy place in the vicinity of a plot is inauspicious. The distance of temple from the plot should be double of its height at least, so that shadow of the temple does not fall on the plot. If any temple exists near any house or plot or even if the shadow of temple is falling on the plot, the resident cannot be happy.

Vriksha Vedh (Trees Obstacle) : There should not be any tree of bargad (banyan), peepal or any other big tree around the plot. The distance between tree and the main gate should be to the extent that the shadow of tree does not fall on it. If the morning sunrays directly fall on the plot the residents of such place would be healthy and happy, and also without any disease.

Vriksha-vedh(tree obstacle) is harmful for health. The vaastu-experts suggest that the tree can be situated on the west of the house so that it remains cool. If there is a well on the plot it should be saved from the afternoon shadow. If such a thing happens the water becomes polluted and smells bad.

Around the house mainly beside the main gate there should be no drains with dirt or dustbin. The East, North or Ishan angle or its surrounding area should be free of any sign board, stone, rock, electric pole, big pillar or cactus plants.

On the west or southern part of the house there should be no pond, river canal, water tank, well, water storage area etc. All these are harmful for the residents of the plot.

According to " Vrihatsanhita" water reservoir is recommended to be situated in northern or north eastern (Ishan) area.

Pradhyadistha salile suthamh shikhimapam Ripupayanchya
Stree Kalaha streedoushtayam Naiswayam vittatmajavid vridhih

—*Vrihadṣanhita.*

It means that if water-source is in the east of a house, then, there is a risk of loss of son, in south-east there is risk of fire, in south there is risk of enemies, in south-west there is risk for woman's tension, in west woman's visibility, in north-west loss of wealth, whereas it is wealth multiplier in north, and in north east it is good for birth of a son.

Vaastu Zameen

Vaastu zameen— According to Vaastu Shastra, that part of land is called as vaastu where a person could build a house for living.

What is described above is a short definition of vaastu. Now the question is that what is the speciality of the " Vaastu zameen" that is selected or why is the piece of land called as " Vaastu zameen"

To know whether a piece of land is " Vastu zameen", or is suitable or not it is important to detect that it is not drowned in the rain-water. If the residential land is drowned by rain-water, then it is not, at all suitable for residential use. To make it suitable for building a house or for any other use, it is filled with soil and its level is raised; and it is left, as it is, for a few years so that it could absorb the water of rain and becomes hard. It would be better if the plot is levelled by a roller in winter season.

The land, the level of which is raised artificially, as said above, is found that the level of water is easy to be attained. So boring water is easily available. But it is also true that the water, found from such land, is salty and harmful for health as it is hard to digest. It is unsuitable for washing clothes. Therefore, for "Vaastu" naturally raised up plot is considered to be best and most suitable.

Due to scarcity of land in Bengal people use to put mud and garbage in ponds, and lake and fill them in a few years. Such land is sold by demarcating plots .

The 'Vaastu'-plot, obtained by such process is not considered good, as its water is contaminated and salty.

Salt lake city, known as a posh residential area was, at a time a big lake of salt and that is the reason why it is called as "Salt Lake city".

In this colony even the millionares living there are facing the problem of drinking water. Each house owner uses his car to bring water from elsewhere for drinking purposes.

Just opposite to this is the Raipur city of M.P. which is a very hot area and the M.G. road area of this city, is situated at a higher plinth of land. We have tasted the water and found it very sweet and tasty.

While drilling for boring, hard stones are found after depth of 12 feet. The land is rocky with very hard stones. The water found is sweet due to hard land. Where atmosphere is hot and intolerable, extremely hot winds blow here. Vaastu shastra's say that water dug out from hard rocks is pure and good. So, a person becomes healthy, even after living in Raipur for a month.

In this way we find that while selecting a piece of land for'vaastu', its level of plinth should be checked. After this the direction of wind is to be checked so, that there is no "Vayu Dosh" (wind defect).

It should be checked that if there is any polluting factory at the north west (Vayavya) of the plot whose pollution is affecting the owner. It is found that if there is any alcohol factory, bricks kiln, cement factory, fertilizer factory or of chemicals in north-west, the resident faces the problem of bad alcoholic smell, cement dust, smoke etc which is highly harmful for health. So many people are affected by the dangerous bricksmoke to the extent of tuberculosis, which I have seen myself.

Therefore, to set up a Colony or a township the piece of land, that is selected, should be examined at its north-west for bad effect of air pollution.

In these directions the wind blows from south to west so 'Vaastu' plot should be selected according to the direction of blowing of wind, otherwise the whole city-folk could fall ill.

We have seen the biggest steel plant of Asia i.e."Bhilai steel plant". This steel plant is situated exactly at the south eastern direction and Bhilai city is situated at north west. Due to this, city is pollution free.

It is so, because the wind blows from north-west towards

south-east, So the hazardous smoke of the plant does not reach the city area.

Therefore the land suitable for'Vaastu' should be checked on all the four sides and all conditions should be precisely considered.

Thus primarily we have discussed about the selection of plot on the basis of level and direction. Now we shall talk about the hardness of the plot.

To select a plot for'Vaastu' the interior inspection of the plot is also important. For this first of all we must check whether there is grass, herbs or trees on the plot or not. It there is a tree of mango, neem, kathal or jamun etc we could understand that the level of water is not very deep and you could find water easily by drilling a bore.

It there are small plants on the land, you should uproot, two three plants together. If the plants are derooted soon, then the plot is not good, if it takes a little effort to take out the plants the plot is so so, and if the plants are hard enough and snatched after a good toil, the plot is then the best one.

After this, you should plant money-plant, bel, or tulsi. Money-plant is very sensitive branch(bel). If money plant flourishes on the plot for a longer period of time, the plot is best one.

The plant of tulsi cultivates only on good land. So if tulsi is so cultivated well on the plot you could conclude that the plot is good enough. According to scientific point of view tulsi is grown only on good land. After this, the plot you have selected, could be further examined as under.

Make a hole on the ground one foot wide, long and deep. After digging the mud that has come out, take that mud and refill the hole. If the hole remains a bit empty the ground or plot is not suitable for 'vaastu' and if suppose mud is left even after filling the hole then the plot is best for 'vaastu'.

After this experiment, you can do another experiment to check the land.

Make a square hole of one and a half foot and of same depth, fill the hole with water, wait for three minutes after watering. If you find the water absorbed completely, then the plot is not at all suitable for 'Vaastu'.

If the water goes down by half foot then the plot is so-so and you could build a house on such a plot.

And in case the water remains as it is the plot is considered to be the best. The building on such a plot would be safe and prosperous forever.

By above experiments, you can detect hardness of soil of a plot.

Now we will pay attention to the colour of the land. Different parts of land are of different colours. According to the colour of the land the selection of plot and the foundation of the building is laid.

White land : The area whose land is found white from distance is considered to be the best land. The foundation on such a land is very strong; the grip of such a land is also very strong and powerful. Almost all the land in Bengal is found white.

Therefore, here the land is fertile hard and strong.Buildings here are also strong. Due to the hardness of land in Bengal the decision of metro train had been taken there.

Red land : Next to white land red land is considered to be good. Such mud or land is generally found at higher and dry areas. Bihar, Uttar pradesh, Delhi, and MP has got red land.

Such kind of land is hard and strong enough. Where there is such kind of land the digging for foundation is not required to be done more deeply. In such soil small stones are found in quantity which is also called "PEBBLES". With the help of 'PEBBLES' foot path (Kachhi sadak) could be made. With pebbles water in rainy days does not spill over on roads.

Black soil : This soil is very very soft generally it is used for making statues and toys. If there is black soil, extra care is to be taken while the foundation of the building is laid. This soil is loosened in rains. Such kind of soil is like gold for the farmers. Such soil is highly suitable for farming. If a building is made on such soil it would not last long.

Soil with Sand : Such soil is not at all suitable for building a house, because there are possibilites of breakage. If you have to use such a land with sand in it, the soil must be first tested. If a building is built on sandy land it could not last very long.

In this way, after testing and identifying the class of soil we could select a piece of land. But its direction must also be perfect according to the principles and rules of "Vaastu shastra".

Vaastu Principle

"Atyant vridhi Nrinami Shanpragudakhalwam.
Anyadekshku plalavam tesham shakhdanthanidam"

—*Narad Compilation*

In the Narad compilation it has been said about the choice of land that the slope of land should be towards the Ishan or North east or east which results into continuous increase of wealth. If the slope of the land is in other direction then it is very harmful.

Therefore after choosing the land for the building of a house it is neccessary to see that the principle of vaastu shastra is applicable or not. If it is not applicable then the land should better be left.

Keeping in mind the inside level of land, the surrounding level of land should be examined carefully.

The base of the land, angle of the plot, shape of the plot, the area of the plot should conform to the vaastu princinple.

Necessary Precautions while choosing plots.

(1) The plot we choose should be square.

(2) Triangular land is not suitable.

(3) If the land is angular but the length and breadth of the land is suitable then the land is faultless.

(4) The land should not have cracks or unevenness.

(5) Slope should be towards North-East Ishan.

(6) If the land does not conform to the vaastu principle it should be better left because it cannot be improved upon.

(7) The circular land is not suitable.

Angle of land

(1) If all the four angles of the land are equal to or of 90° then it is said to be the best angle.

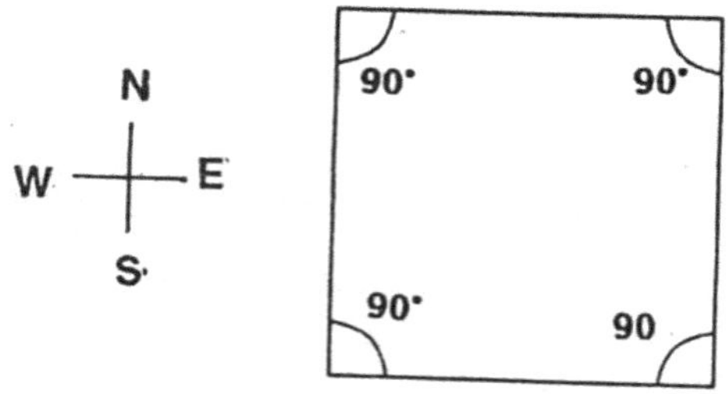

(2) The angle of South West should be of 90°.

(3) North-West angle should be of 90° or more than 90°but not less than 90° in any case.

(4) South-East angle should be at least of 90° or more than 90°but not less than 90°.

(5) North East angle should be of 90°or less than 90°but not more than 90°in any case.

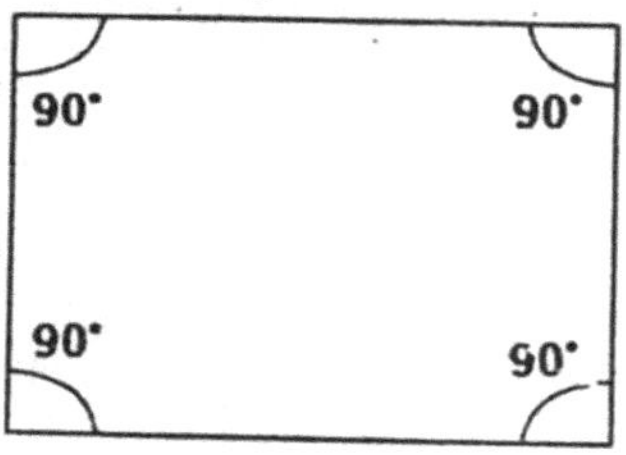

Rectangular with four right angles and. breadth & length should be less than 1:2.

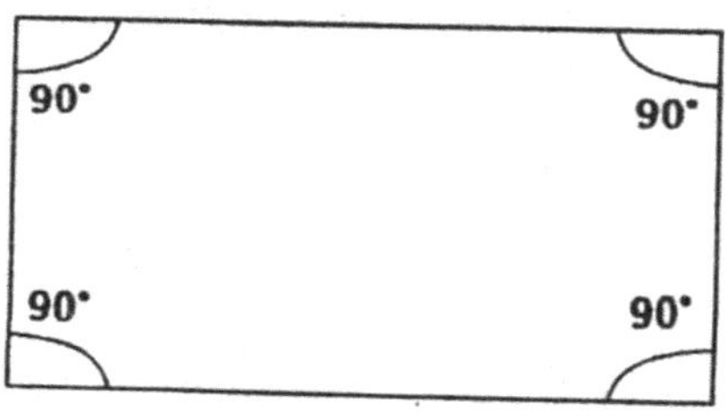

Rectangular with four right angles and. breadth & length to the maximum 1:2

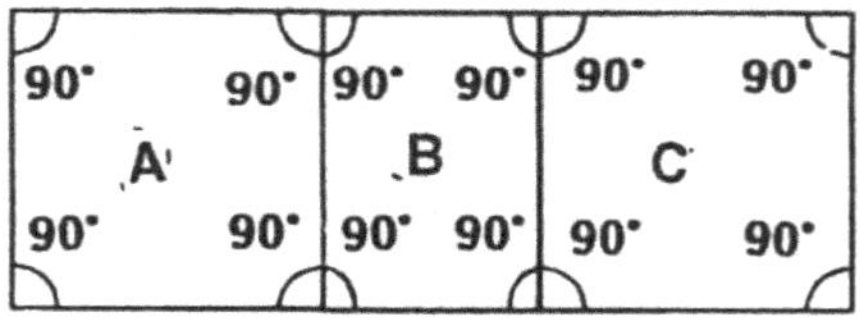

A. The plot is square with 90° angle.

B. The plot is square with 90° angle but is smaller than the A & C plots. This plot, which is between the two plots is narrow, is not good.

C. This plot is of 90° angle which is equal to the plot A.

Gain-Loss from the above angles.

(1) If the slope of land is in the Ishan and East direction, then it is very profitable.

(2) If the plot is down in the East then Lakshmi lives there; if in Agnaya angle : grief, in South-angle : death, in Nairithya-angle: fear, in west-angle : quarrel, in wayava-angle : death, in North-angle : family increase; in Ishan-angle : gem accumulation.

(3) The middle high plot is very bad. It gives problems to the landlord. Beside this, the landlord becomes a victim of the

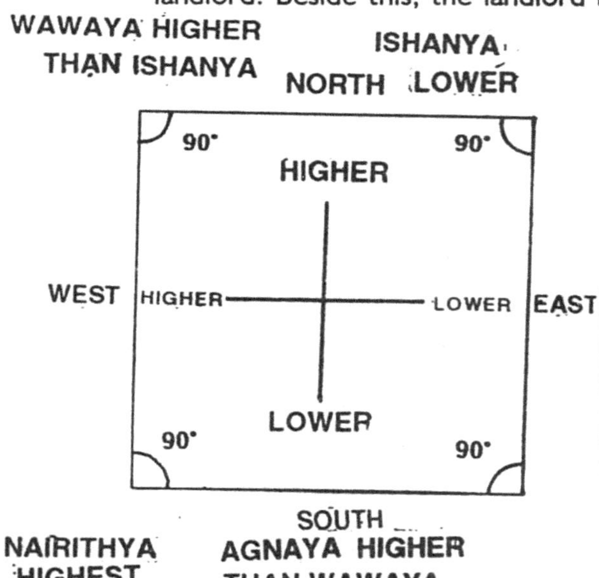

(4) The plot with slope in the South gives death from disease. This plot should be high from the North.

(5) The plot which is low at the middle and high from all the sides is enemy killer.
(6) Nairithaya angle holds the highest place among the plots.
(7) The West part should be higher than East.
(8) Agnaya angle should be a little bit higher than the Wayava angle.
(9) Wayava angle is higher than the Ishan angle.
(10) Some Vastu Shastri have suggested that the both Agnaya angle & the Wayava angle should be same.

Increase & Decrease of plot Angle.

Sometime there is an increase and decrease in the plot angle which effects the plot, therefore, such increase and decrease of the plot angle should be kept in mind. If the angle increases towards the North and East that is the best angle. Beside this all angles should be equal; specially the South- West angle should be of 90°. There should be no fault in this parameter.

The maximum ratio of length & breadth of the plot should be 2 : 1 and not more than that. Therefore the length should not exceed the breadth beyond the ratio.

The stretch in the North-East is said to be good. The stretch in any other direction should be first purified & then used.

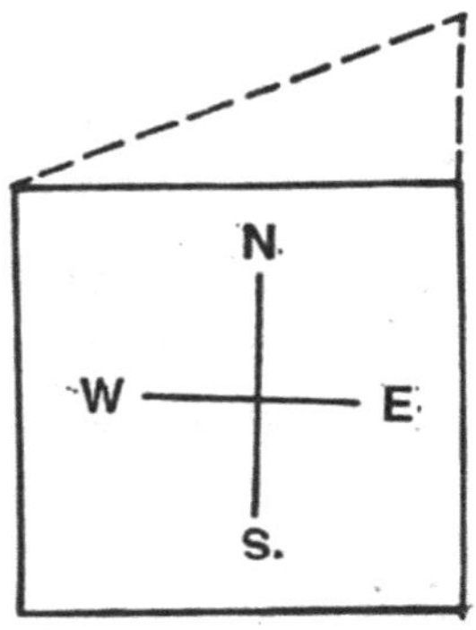

The stretch from North to Ishan angle is best.

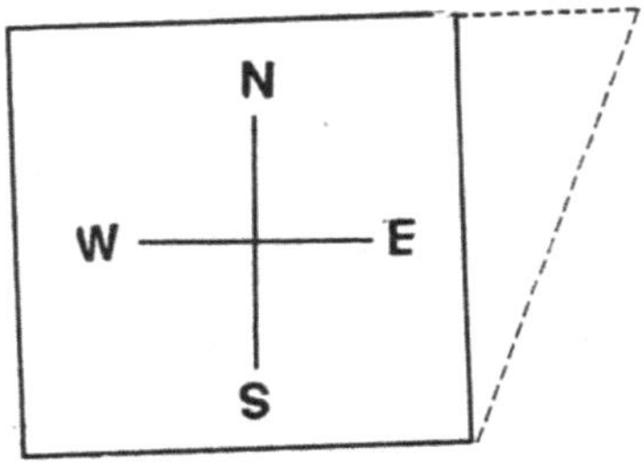

The increase from North and East to the Ishan angle is the best for plot.

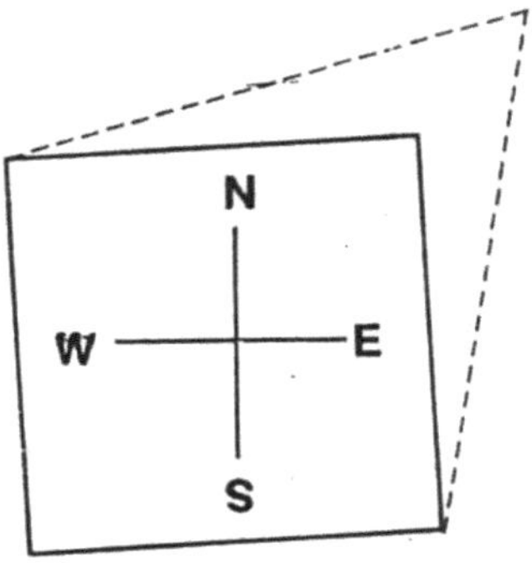

The increase of Ishan area to North & East is the best for the plot.

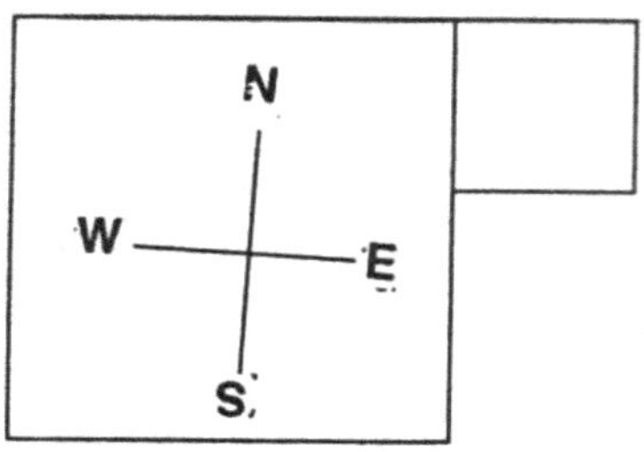

The square increase of Ishan angle to the East is the best for the plot.

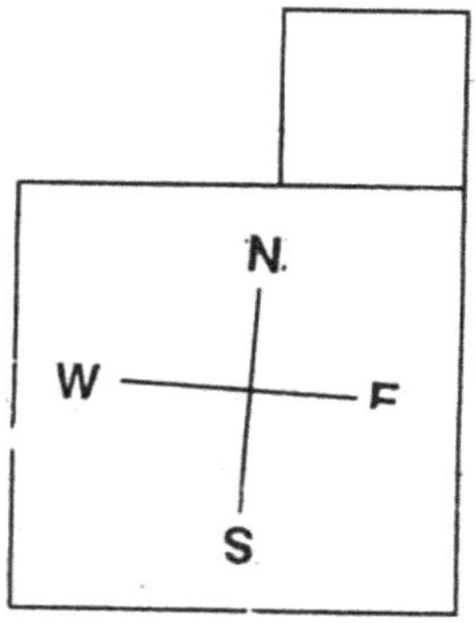

The square increase of Ishan angle to the North is said to be the best.

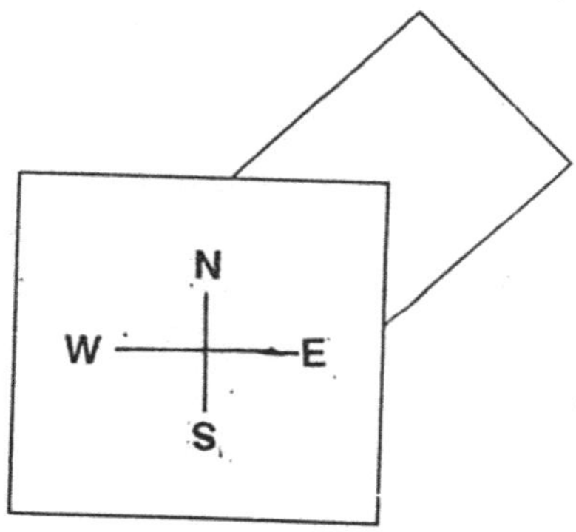

The square increase in North and East to the Ishan angle is said to be the best plot.

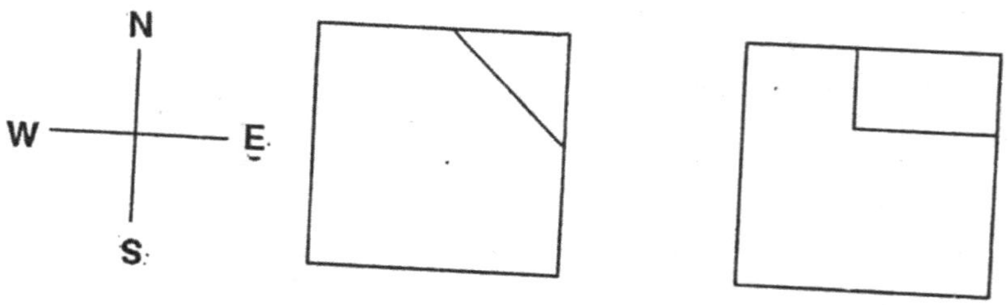

If there is a cut on inside of the plot in the Ishan angle then it is not of a good category. The Landlord does not enjoy happiness and there is an obstacle in the progress of the family.

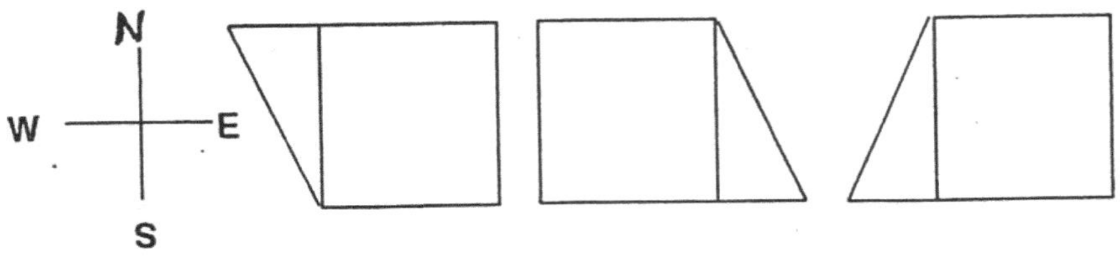

The increased angles in Wayava, Nairithaya and Agnaya are not good. If they are straightened upto angle of 90° then they are faultless.

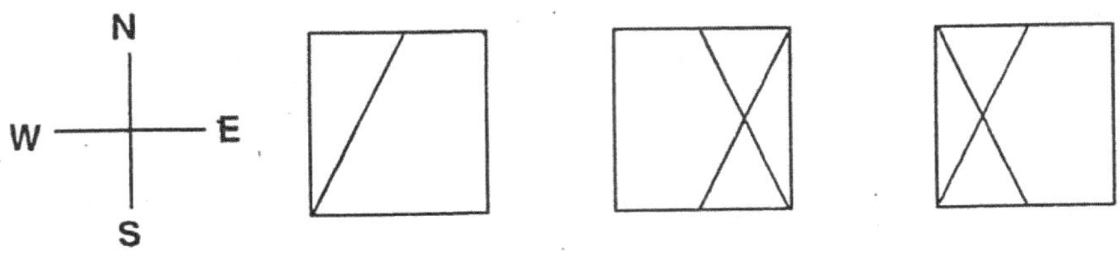

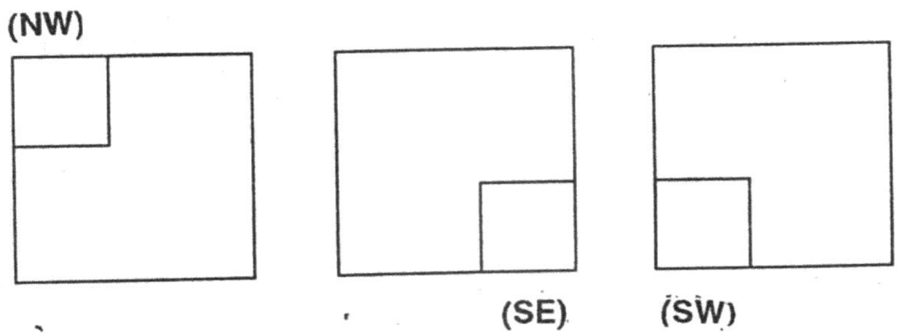

The square and triangle angles of the Wayava and Agnaya and Nairithaya towards the inside are rarely found; which is not a suitable plot. These plots should be corrected by straightening them at the 90° angle.

"Shurmahal" had written in his book "Rajmartand" that some plots are of such shape that they are advised not to be purchased, though the sizes and position of those are good. Therefore the angles and direction are very effective to the luckiness of the plot.

Entrance & Direction

According to entrance the face of the plot should be in which direction, is very essential to look at. East and North faced plot is said to be the best quality of plot. West and South faced plots are kept in the ordinary category.

If the face of the plot is towards the West and South then while building a house, we have to maintain certain care. We give following suggestions & instructions to the Architect only then he should make a good plan according to the technical viewpoint keeping in mind the direction and the position of the plot.

Worship Room	Ishan or North East
Kitchen	Agnaya or South East
Bath room	East
Sleeping room	South-West
Dining hall	West
Toilet	South or South West
Animal house	North-West
Locker	North
Oil,Ghee or any liquid	East or South-East
Study room	West or South-West
Entrance door	East

Garden	North
Well, water reservoir, Taps & water tank	Ishan or North-East
Water going drain	Wayava or North West
Septic Tank	Wayava or North West
Sitting Room	Agnaya or South East
Open Lawn	Ishan or North East
Windows	According to ratio
Doors	According to ratio
Ventilators	In every room which opens towards the outside.

Location of Well

In any village, colony or building the well should not be in the Agnaya Nairithaya & Wayava angle. Digging well in such a prohibited place does not augur well for the inmates living at such a place. Leaving all these three angles, the well should be built in Ishan, North or East direction. There are some rules and precautions :—

(1) The well should be in the East and North direction.

(2) If a well is in the North, then it should be a little bit towards the East.

(3) If a well is in the East, then it should be shifted a little towards the North.

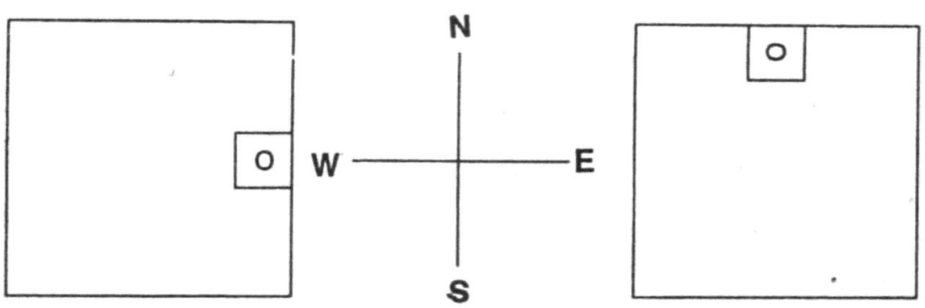

The well built in the East and North direction of the plot gives peace.

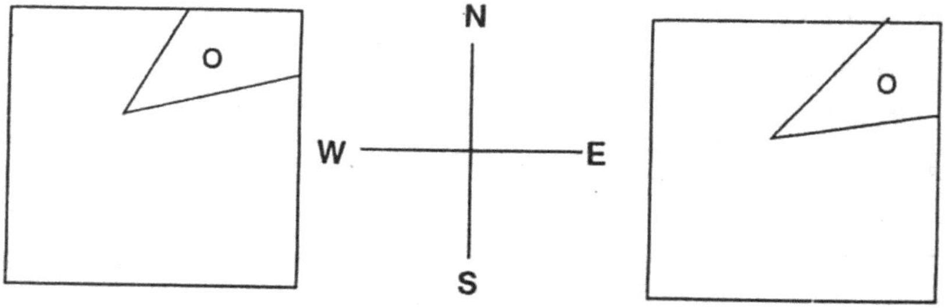

North & East shifted wells are of best category and the man, using this well is of contented nature.

(4) There should be no well in the middle of the plot though some people like such a well to be built even if it is not good. It is the sign of quarrel.

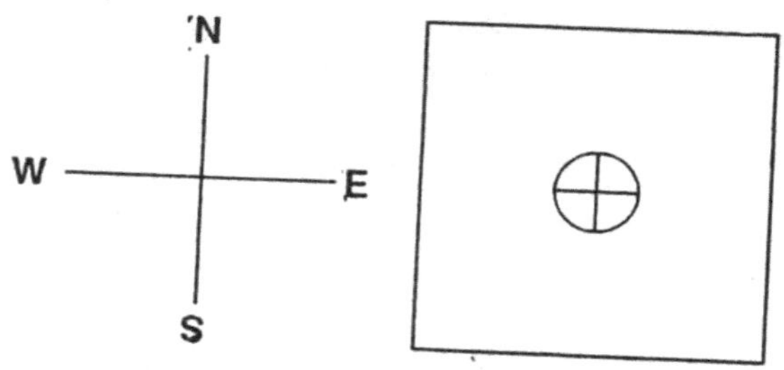

(5) The wells made in the West and South directions are not good.

(6) If a well is in South East— Agnaya or in North West-Wayava direction then it is not good.

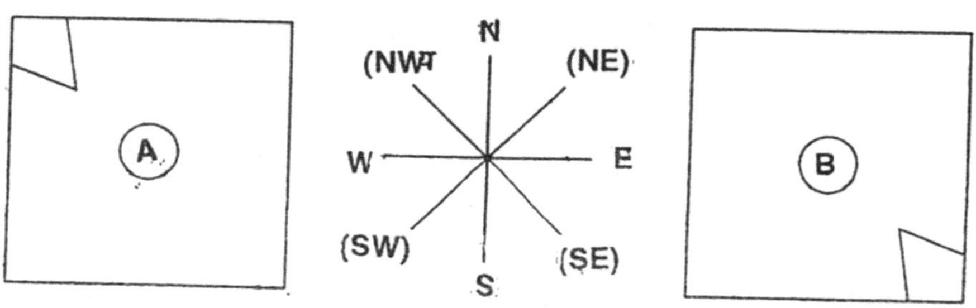

(a) If a well is dug up in Wayava and Nairithya west bound

angle, then the resident will suffer from enemy, bad health, loss of wealth and tension between husband and wife.

(b) Well in East Agnaya or South Agnaya angle are not good. The people who live here suffer from blood pressure and bad health.

(7) If a well is just opposite the direction of the main gate or entrance, it is said not to be good.

(8) One should keep in mind that the well should be circular above the ground, it can be square or circular below the ground. If a well is not circular above the ground & is square in the Ishan angle then it has bad effect and it is not auspicious from the vaastu point of view.

Vaastu House Construction

To construct a house we have to choose a plot first according to the vaastu shastra, after choosing the plot it should be purified by vedic customs. After worshipping the land, the coustruction work of house should be started.

Till now you have studied about the land, direction etc before building a house as detailed in the vaastu shastra; as to how the soil should be, what type of land should be, what should be the shape of the plot? Now we will tell you about what is vaastu building, its principles and how to build it?

First of all, you should clear the plot and the surrounding land of the plot on which you want to construct house. If it is possible to clear the double the area of the plot surrounding the plot in which the house is to be built we should clear it; because vedh-fault lies to that double area.

First of all, we should build a boundary wall all along the plot. This boundary wall should be built on an auspicious occasion. The boundary wall should be started from the Nairithaya to the Wayava side; After that, it should be from Agnaya to Ishan side and from Wayava to Ishan side. As water is very essential for the building construction hence water facility should be provided in the Ishan side after the boundary wall is completed.

Now pipe water is very much in demand in the modern world as more water is drawn out from less land. Special attention should be given that the height & breadth of the boundary walls of South and West should be higher than the North & East boundary walls.

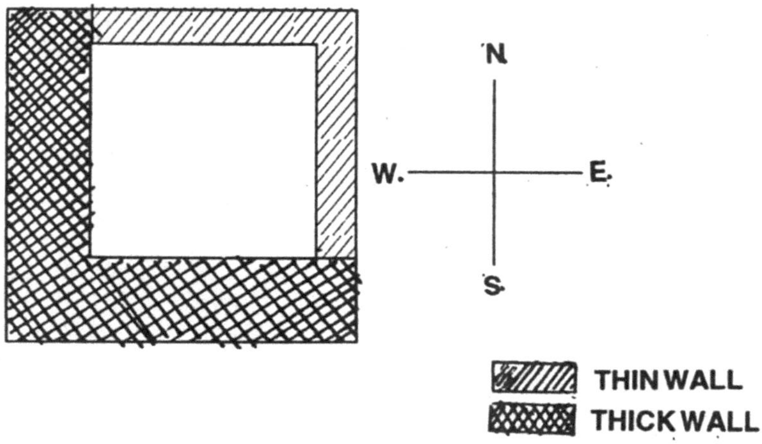

The wall of West & South should be thicker than the East & North wall, as shown in the figure according to vaastu.

While making the wall the work should be started from the South West side and it should proceed to South East while working and it should go on working towards North West and afterwards towards the South-East to North-East and from North-West to North-East.

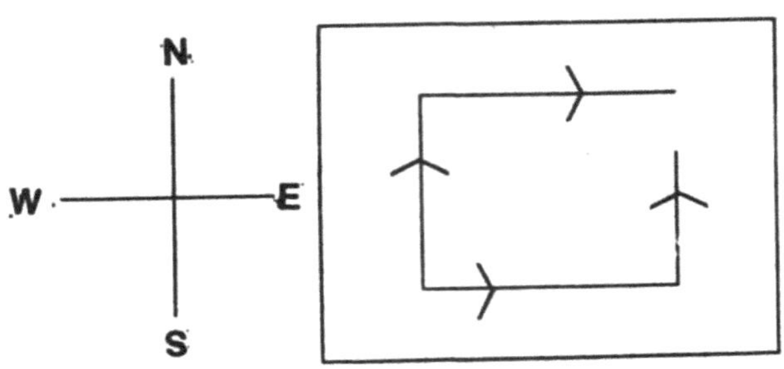

The construction should conform to the figure. After completing the construction of the boundary wall, the water arrangement should be made. After that the house construction should be started.

If you want to build a underground cellar then it should be built before the construction of house. Cellar is very important. Cellar is the first item after foundation of the house. Therefore this should be within the vaastu rules.

Underground Cellar

This is the first construction of the house. You should know one thing first that vaastu shastra does not allow the construction of the cellar as it is very mysterious— It exhibits mysteriousness of the house.

If it is very neccessary to build a cellar then it should be built in North & East side of the plot. It should never be built in the South and West directions. The entrance of the cellar should be in North & East direction and it should be open if possible.

You should remember that cellar should not be in the middle of the vaastu plot.

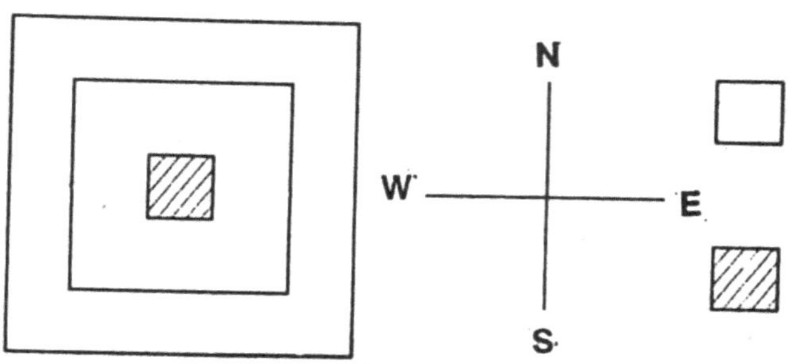

Place of house construction.

Cellar in the middle of house is not good.

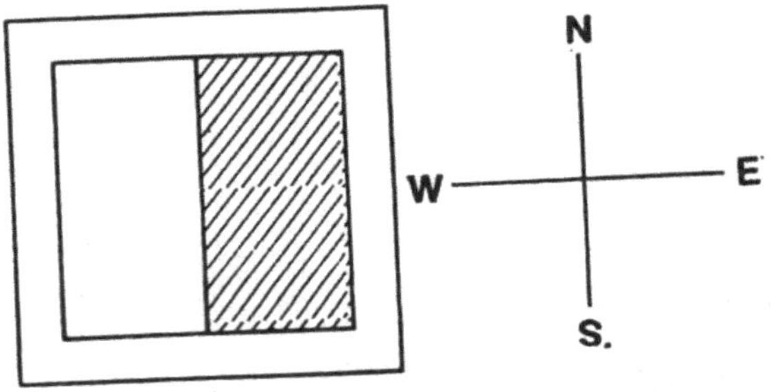

Place of cellar construction. It should be in the East direction.

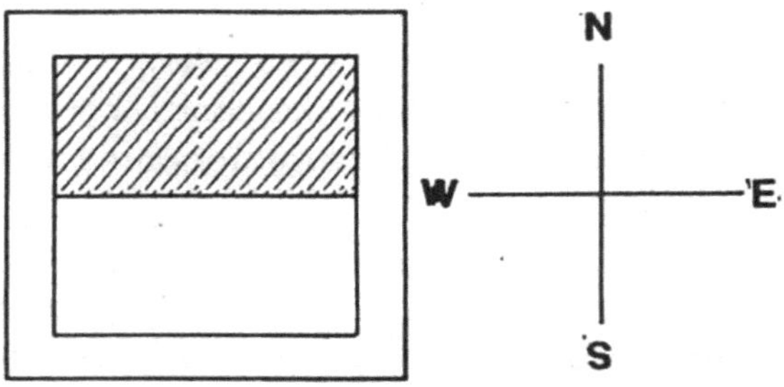

Place of cellar construction. In the North-side of building it is alright.

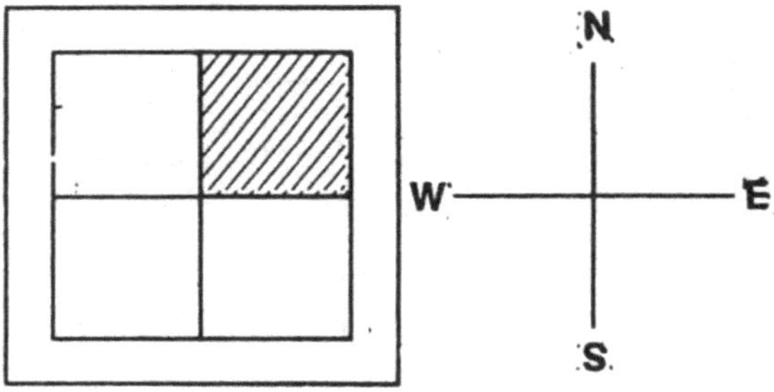

Place of cellar construction. North-East side is good for cellar building.

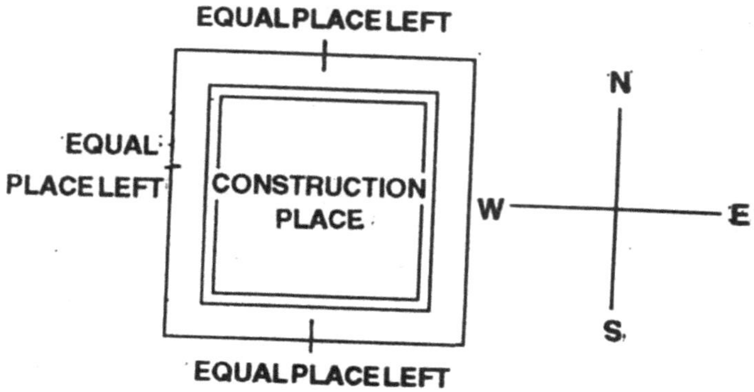

Equal space should be left while constructing the house in the plot.

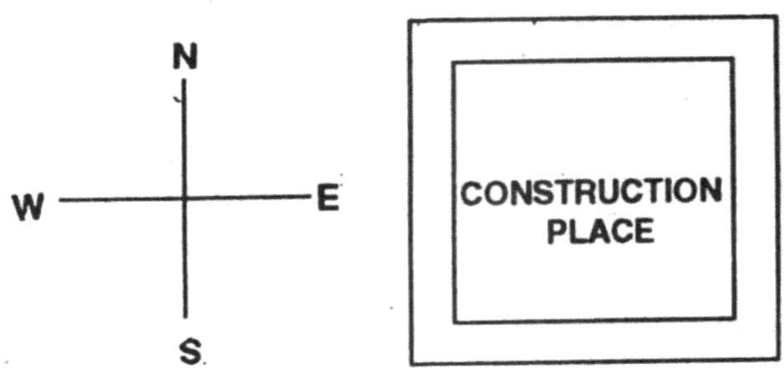

More place should be left in the North and East direction than the South & West side. This is good for house construction and the people residing there are free from debt problems.

Construction Direction of Vaastu House.

According to the Vaastu, the Vaastu construction holds an important place in the house construction. There are many beliefs about the direction to start the construction of the Vaastu house.

But I have experiences that if the construction starts from the South- West then it meets a happy ending. After starting from South West it can go on to other directions.

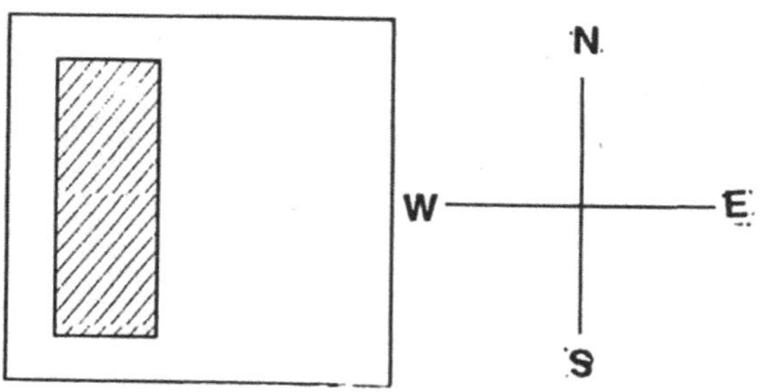

One room Vaastu construction— This construction starts from the West and it is a good construction.

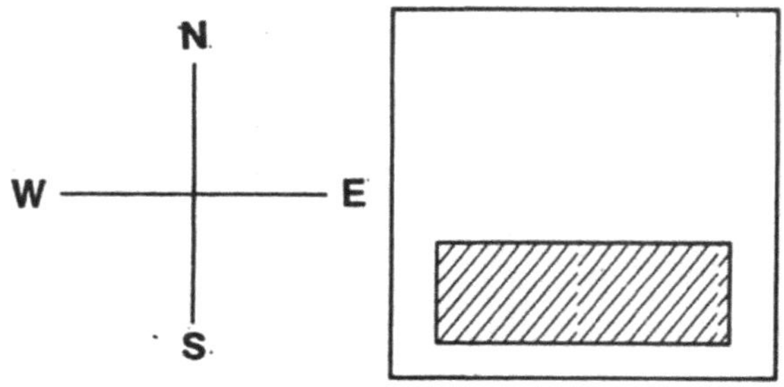

One room Vaastu construction—This construction starts from the South direction. This construction is of best category.

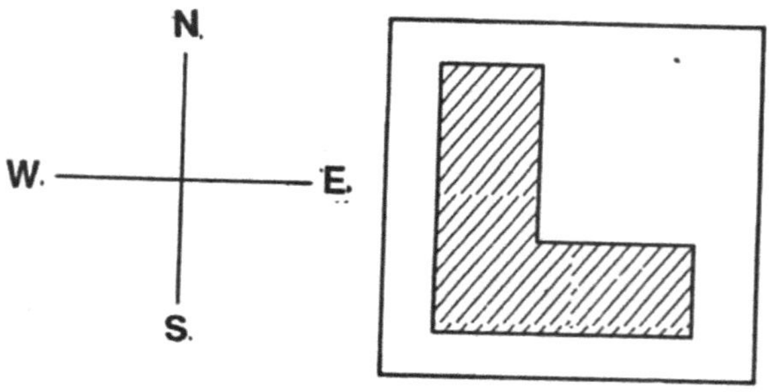

Two room Vaastu construction—This construction starts from the South West and is a good construction.

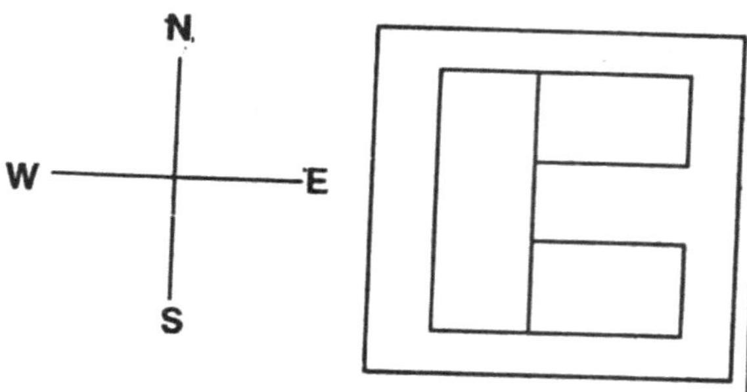

Construction from South West & North direction—This type of construction gives health, son,& peace to the family.

Faulty Construction.

The construction with fault gives harmful results to the landlord and its family members. Therefore, we should save ourselves from the faulty construction.

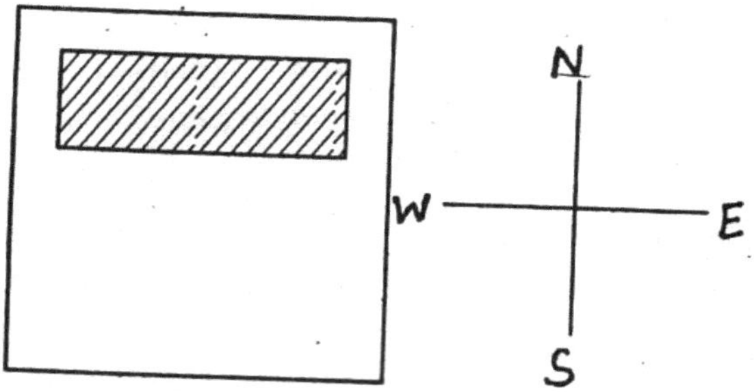

North direction construction is faulty.

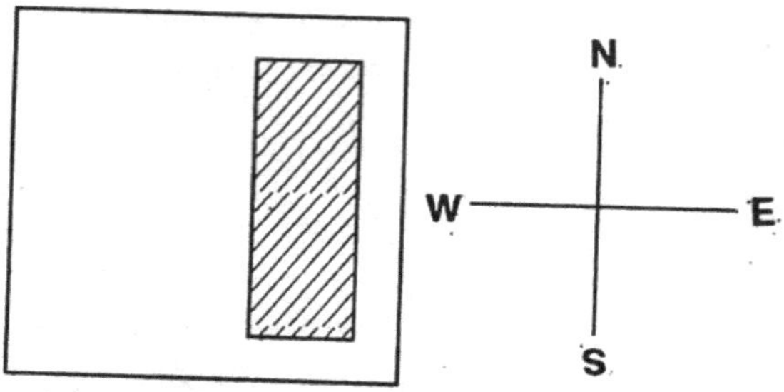

East direction construction is faulty.

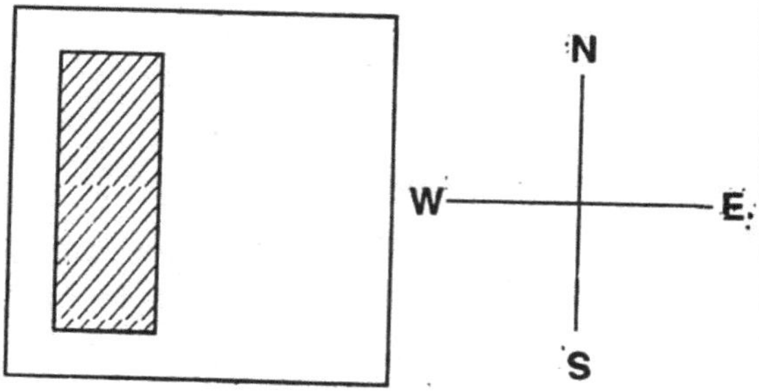

West direction construction is faulty.

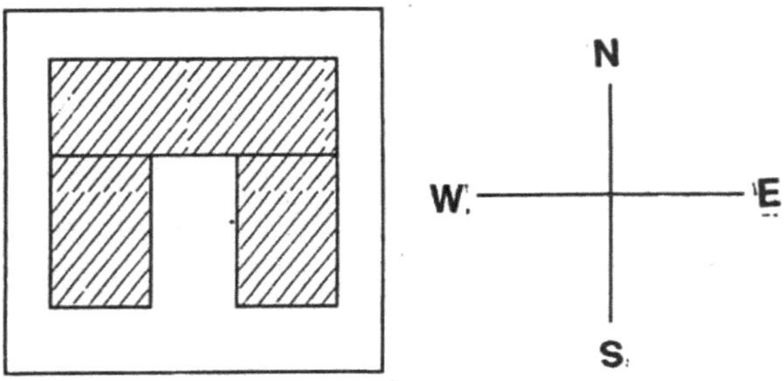

This type of construction is called "Chulli Trishal Vaastu". which destroys wealth.

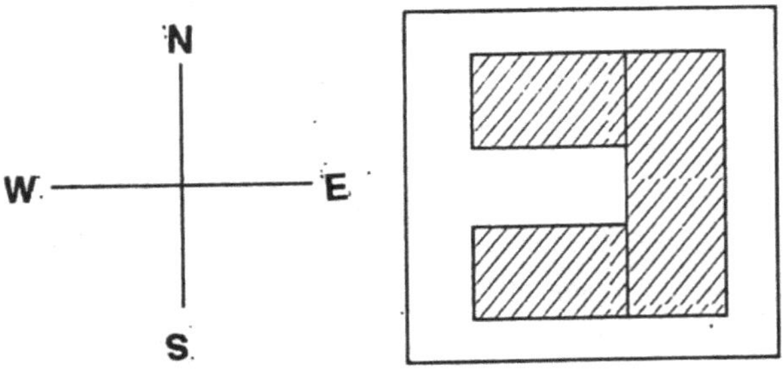

This construction is called "Pakhshadhan Trishal Vaastu" which leads to son's death and makes more enemies.

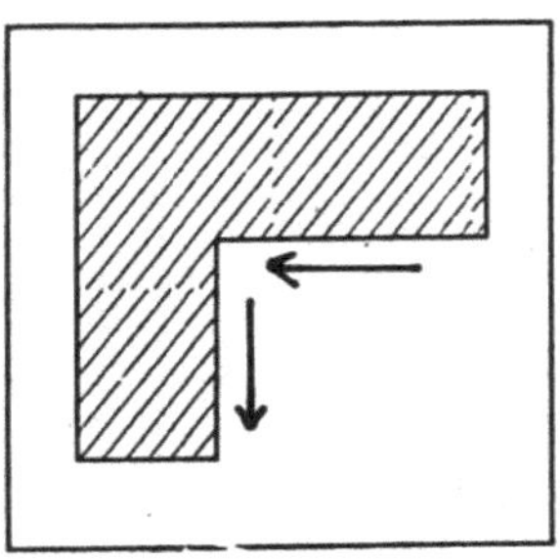

This construction is called "Yam Surya Dwishala Vaastu" This type of construction attracts State punishments and even accounts for death sentence of the owner.

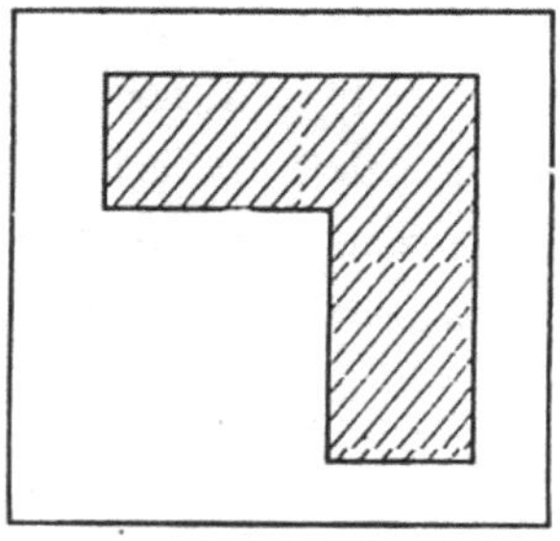

This construction is called "Dand 'Dwishala Vaastu" due to which the landlord always get penalty for every work and he also gets punishment physically from the State.

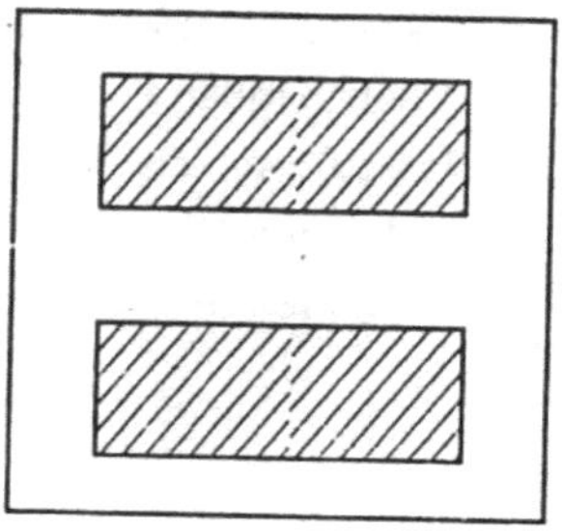

This construction is called "Glass Dwishala Vaastu". This construction gives mental and physical agony to the landlord. His friends go away from him & he becomes lonely.

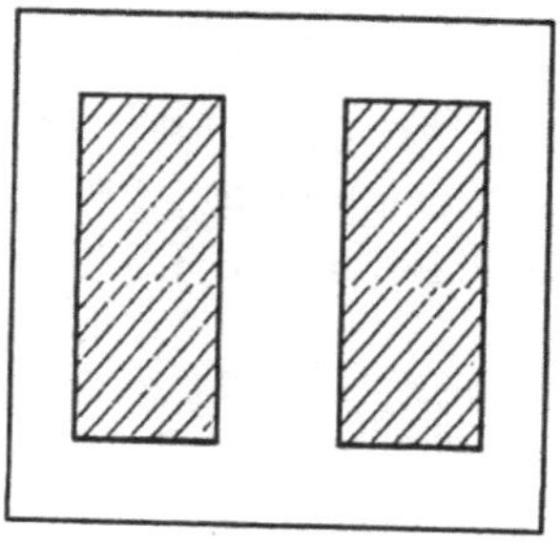

This construction is called "Grah Chulli Dwishala Vaastu". The people residing are rendered poor immediately.

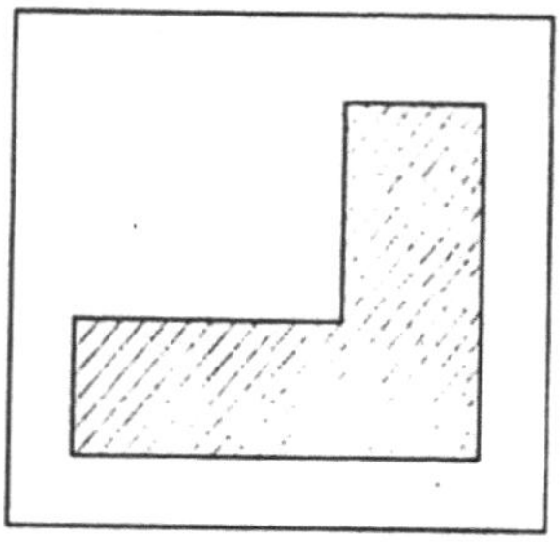

This construction is called "Vaat Dwishala Vaastu" The people residing here suffer from the diseases of gout and wind.

Till now we have seen that the construction on land should be started from which side, which is the lucky construction and which is the unlucky one.

In an ancient holy book "Vishwakarma Prakash" there is a beautiful sanskrit couplet about the construction of interior portions of the house, i.e. how it should be done according to one's neccessity.

Ishanaya Devtageh purvshaya shenmandirem.
Agnaya Podsadan, bhandaragamuthera.
Agnaya Purvayamadhaya dathe manyan mandir.
Agnaya pretashayu madhaya ajayegahe proshethe.
yamayanarithaya madhaya purishkayag mandirum.
Nairithayambpaynmadhaya vidhayabhayasya mandirum.
Paschemmanileyamadhaya Roduarth girish simiritham.
Nathayanatheryamodhaya ratigirich prashesya.
Vtarsnaya madhaya Awasdharth tukaryat.
Nairithayam suthka geh niripana bhumimichattam.

(Viswakarma Prakash)

According to this sanskrit rhyme worship room should be in Ishan, the place of churning out curd should be between the Agnaya and East. Between Agnaya and South should be the place of keeping ghee. Toilet in South and Nairithaya; study room in Nairithaya & West, mourning room should be in West & Wayu angle; husband & wife room in the middle of Wayava & North and delivery room in the Nairithaya.

Construction of building

According to the Vaastu Shastra we can make a house looking at the diagram obeying the laws of the sanskrit rhyme.

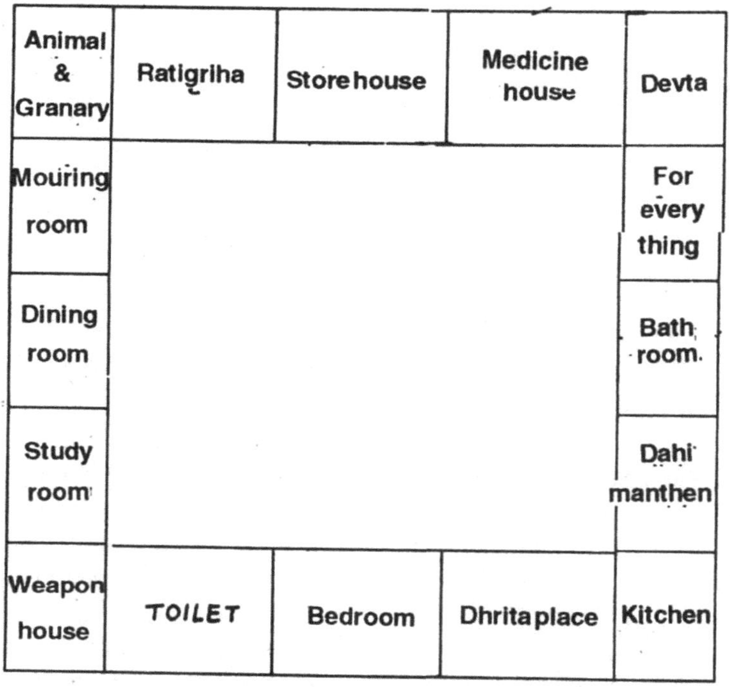

There had been abundant land when this sanskrit rhyme was composed. The rooms which had been shown in the diagram were very important. The society was maintained according to its principles.

But, in the modern world, the circumstances have totally changed, so we make rooms with our neccessity, keeping in view the old feelings & sentiments of the Vaastu law. For example, we donot need a whole room for keeping weapons but we do use that room for keeping generator, machinery things and other such items in that room. For keeping animal a room is useless today, so we use that room for children.

Just like that we change the mourning room into the guest-room. Bathroom & toilet should be made at separate place for the healthy body. While making all the rooms, we should keep in mind the laws of Vaastu construction. Where, when, which room should be built, has to be according to Vaastu-laws —

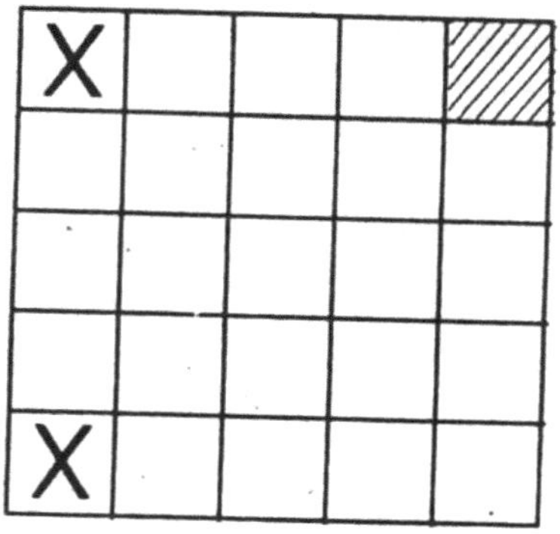

 The best suitable place for the worship room.

X Not good for worship place.

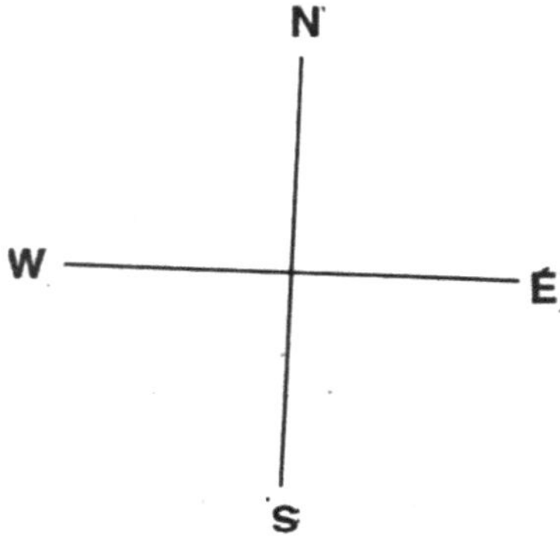

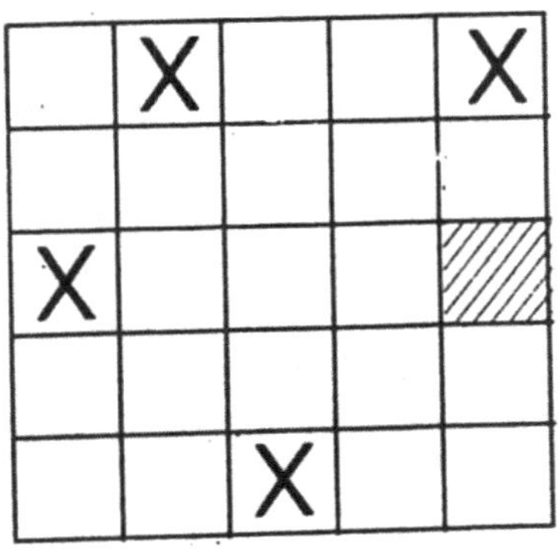

 Good for bathroom construction.

X The landlord will have some problem if bathroom is constructed here.

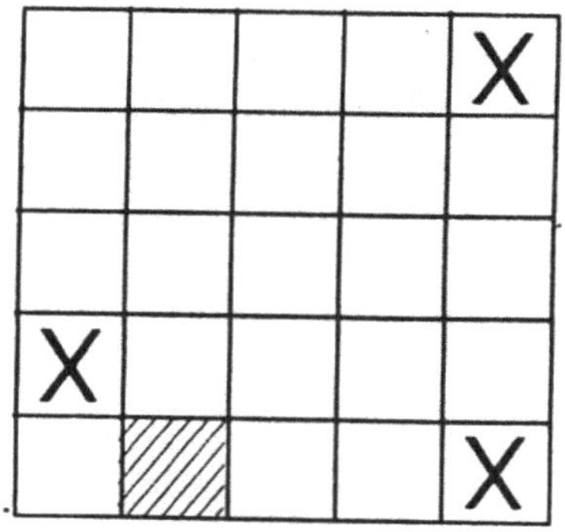

 Suitable for toilet construction.

X Suffers from many problems if toilet is constructed here.

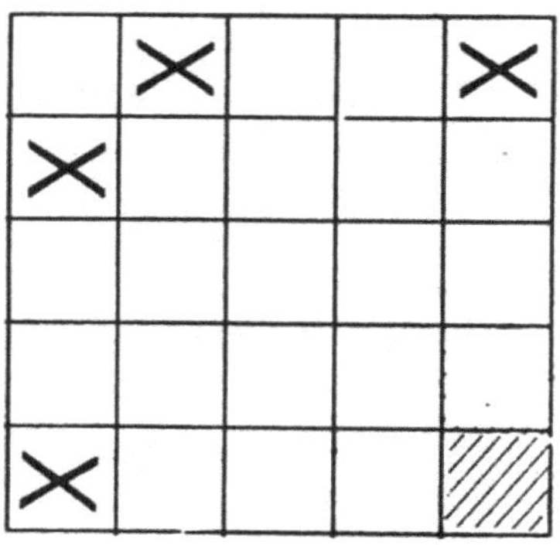

 Good for making kitchen.
Not suitable for kitchen.

X The food will not taste good & the females will fall ill if kitchen is constructed here.

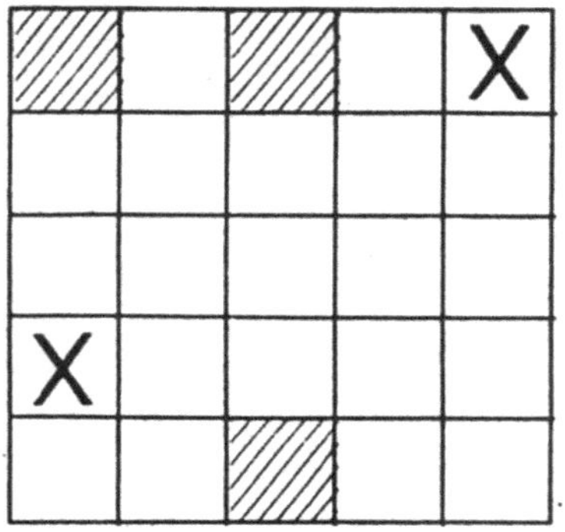

Good for family storehouse.

X Not suitable for storehouse construction.

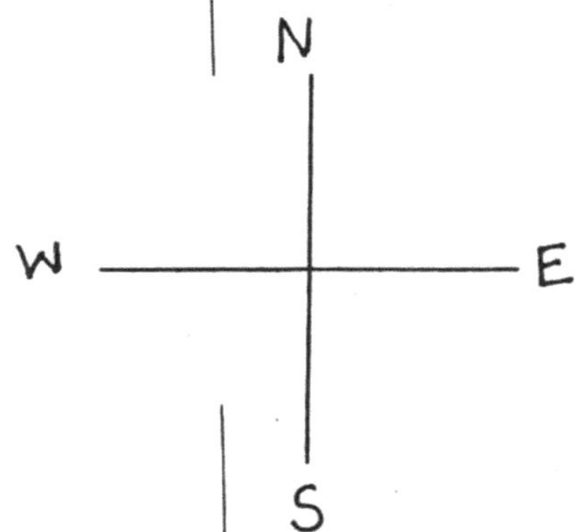

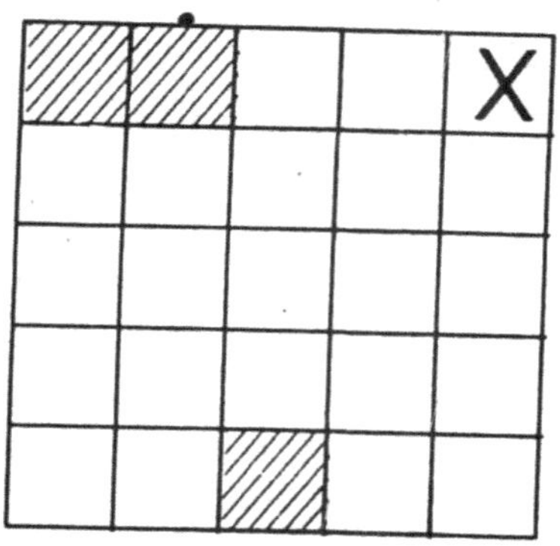

Best suitable place for sleeping rooms.

X Not suitable for sleeping rooms and people will have to incur displeasure of Gods.

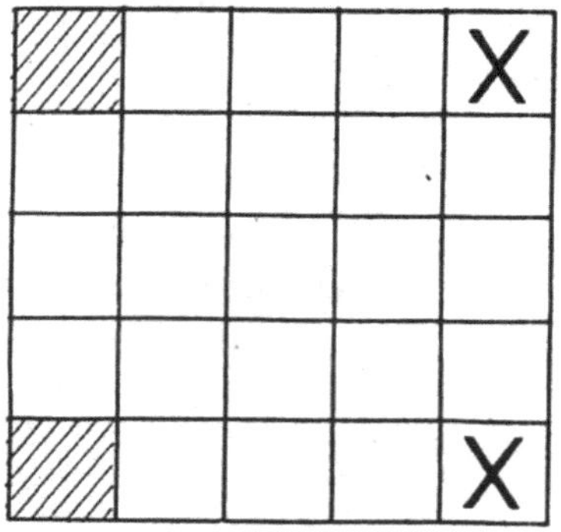

Suitable place for guest room & children room.

X Not good for guestroom & children's room.

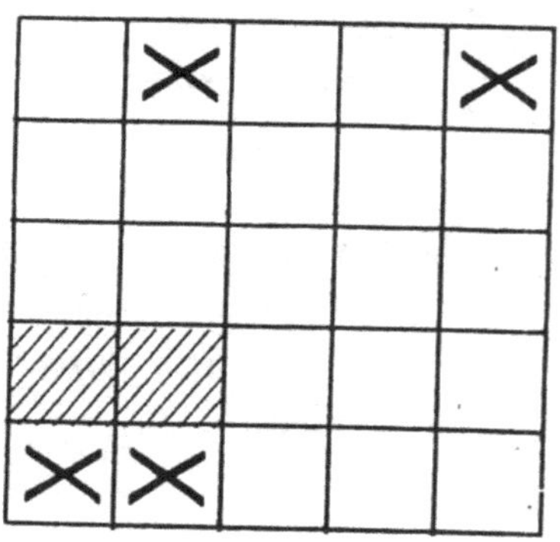

Suitable for study-room.

X Not good for study-room.

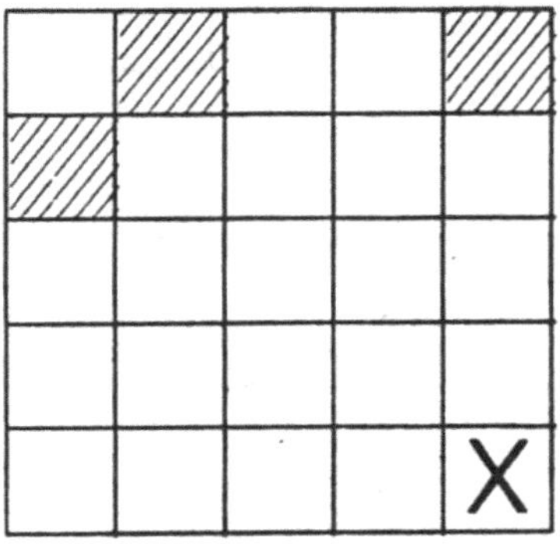

Very suitable for overhead water tank.

X Not suitable for water tank.

This way I have explained you to make which room and where on your plot and this is a matter of an ordinary knowledge. We have tried here that you do not have any problem, while constructing your house. Besides this, if you want to have some more knowledge, then you can consult any Vaastu Shastri and avail of his help.

We discuss now about the stair cases. Staircase is very essential in every house whether it is single floor or double floor. The construction of the stairs should be in such a way that the face of the stairs should be in East or South direction i.e. the stairs should be in West or North side of the house. Beside this, there should be a strong door one each on the upper & lower ends of the stairs, The upper door of the stairs should be equal or less higher than the lower door of the stair.

One should keep in mind that the height of the room above the stairs should not exceed the height of its South West part. The number of stairs should be in odd-numbers, and never in even-numbers. Odd number of steps is considered auspicious for the mansion. Surface of the stairs should always be rough and uneven.

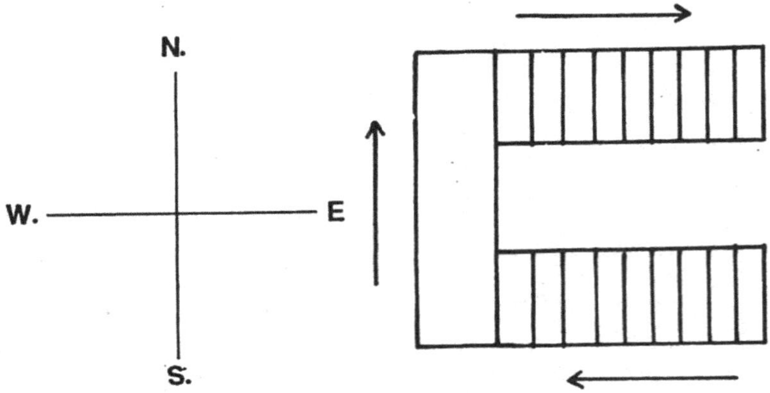

Here the number of steps is nine which is odd and the front of the stair is facing East.

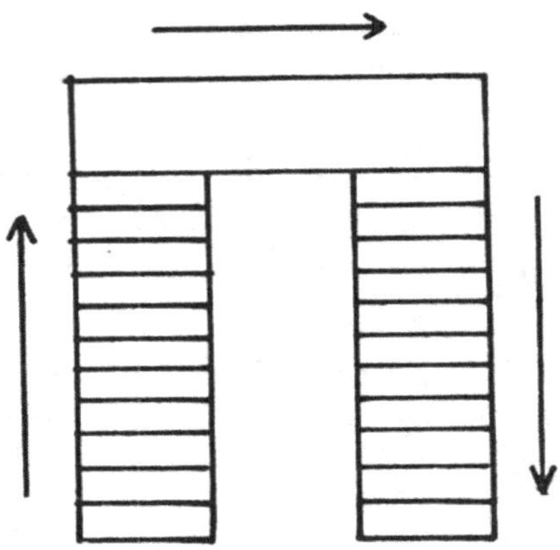

The number of steps is eleven which is odd and the face of the stair is in South.

Royal or Main Door

The first thing to think about main gate or royal door or entrance door of the house is as to where to be constructed or in which direction is to be constructed, after purchasing the land for the house. This is also true that according to the high costs now-a-days, the people make the main door according to direction of the roads going around the plot.

Therefore, we have to keep in mind the direction while purchasing the plot. According to the Vaastu-shastra the construction of the main door of the house should be done, after inspecting the abode of 32 gods residing all around the plot.

Vaastu door is made after seeing the position of God and its fruitful result after dividing the each direction into eight parts. There is a diagram to show all these.

In the wheel of the Vaastu door there are thirty two parts. In these parts the God lives according to their order are which :—

(1) Shikhi, (2) Paryant, (3) Jayant, (4) Indra,
(5) Surya, (6) Satya, (7) Mrish, (8) Aakash,
(9) Vayu, (10) Pusha, (11) Vithetat, (12) Vrihant,
(13) Yam, (14) Gandharva, (15) Bhringraj, (16) Mrig,
(17) Pitre, (18) Dauwarik, (19) Sugreeva, (20) Pushapdatt,

(21) Warun, (22) Asur, (23) Shone, (24) Paap,
(25) Rog, (26) Ahi, (27) Mukhaya, (28) Bhallat,
(29) Som, (30) Bhujang, (31) Aditi, (32) Diti.

32 Parts of Vaastu Door wheel :—

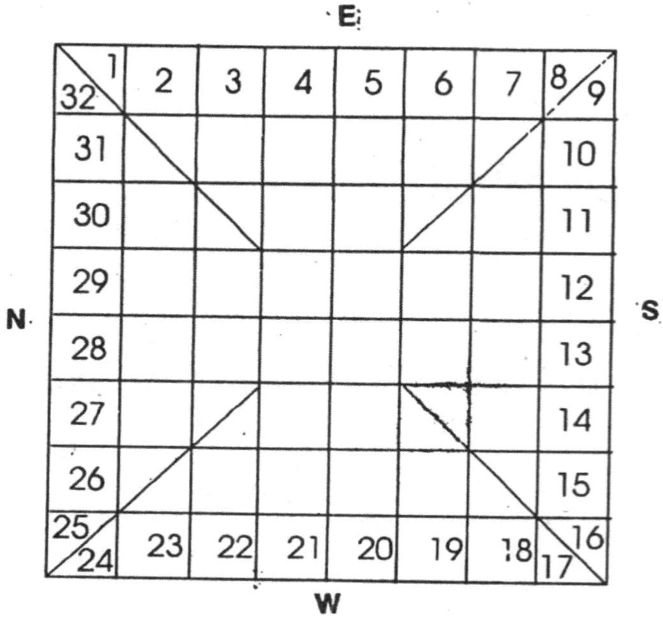

According to the direction the result of **different Gods** are as following-

East Direction Door Constructed

Direction	**Results**
(1) Shikhi direction	Fear of fire.
(2) Paryant direction	Increase in the number of girl child.
(3) Jayant direction	Great profit of money.
(4) Indra direction	Gets royal pleasure.
(5) Surya direction	Increases anger.
(6) Satya direction	Increases telling lies.
(7) Mrish direction	Cruelty
(8) Aakash direction	Fear of theft.

South Direction Door Constructed

(9) Vayu direction	Decrease in child birth.
(10) Pusha direction	Leads to servitude.
(11) Vithetat direction	Leads to vileness (meanness).
(12) Vrihant direction	Adds to son's birth.
(13) Yam direction	Increase in fear.
(14) Gandharva direction	Causes poverty.
(15) Bhringraj direction	Leads to son's lowered prowess.

West Direction Door Constructed

(16) Mrig direction	Son's bravery is lost.
(17) Pitre direction	Short life & gets poor.
(18) Dauwarik direction	More expenditure.
(19) Sugreeva direction	Loss of money.
(20) Pushapdatt direction	Addition of money.
(21) Warun direction	Gain of yoga (luck).
(22) Asur direction	Fear of royalty.
(23) Shone direction	Increase of illness.
(24) Paapyaskhma direction	Accumulation of sin.

North Direction Door Constructed

(25) Rog direction	Fear of being slaughtered.
(26) Ahi direction	More enemies.
(27) Mukhaya direction	Gain of male child & money.
(28) Bhallat direction	Gain of Laxmi (wealth).
(29) Som direction	Progress of religious affair & modesty.
(30) Bhujang direction	Enmity with son.
(31) Aditi direction	Wickedness in ladies.
(32) Diti direction	Becomes poor.

According to the above description we know that main door is made hardly according to the Vaastu-point and while making front door, one must carefully adhere to norms and safeguards, as directed by Vaastu-concept.

According to the Bodhchakram we can show them as following.

EAST	1 Shiki	2 Paryant	3 Jayant	4 Indra	5 Surya	6 Satya	7 Mrish	8 Aakash
	Fear of Fire	More of female	More Money	Royal treat-ment	Anger	More lies	Cruelty	Theft
SOUTH	9 Vayu	10 Pusha	11 Vithetat	12 Vrithant	13 Yam	14 Gandharva	15 Bhringraj	16 Mrig
	Less Children	Servant	Mean ness	More Son	Fear	Poverty	Son's Weakness	Son's bravery lost
WEST	17 Pitre	18 Dau-warik	19 Sugreeva	20 Pushap datt	21 Warun	22 Asur	23 Shone	24 Paap
	Short life	Wastage	Loss of money	Increase of money	Yoga (Luck)	Royal fear	Illness	Collection of sin
NORTH	25 Rog	26 Ahi	27 Mukhaya	28 Bhallat	29 Som	30 Bhujang	31 Aditi	32 Diti
	Murder	Fear of enemy	Male child	Laxmi	Modesty	Enmity	Fault in female	Loss of money

Beside this some Vaastu Shastris had devised new ways of placing the main gate for which there are very simple methods.

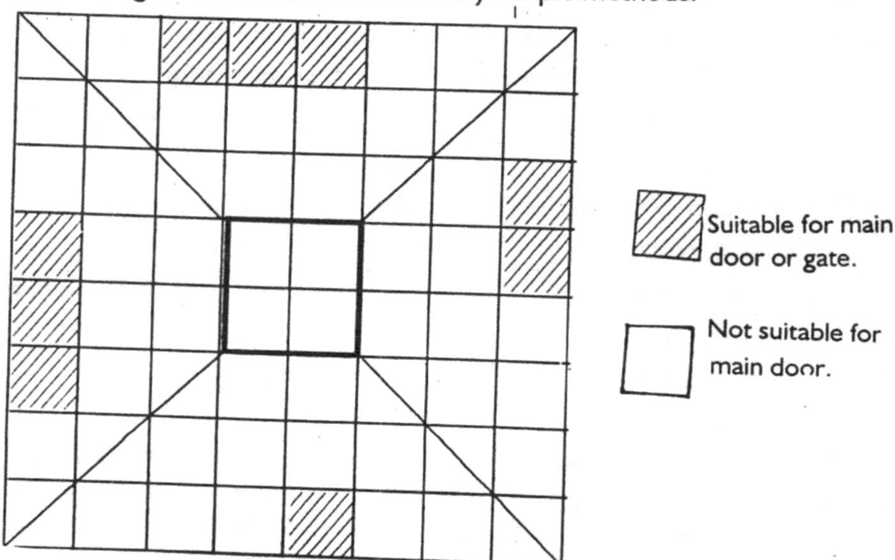

According to the above figure one has to divide each direction into eight parts & then plan out the best place for the main door. One should keep in mind that while standing on the main door the central four blocks or the courtyard should not come in view at the outset.

It has been seen that, while constructing temple, the Bodh chakram principle should be applied. The place in the Bodh chakram which gives auspicious results should be selected for the main door.

In chakram, the East direction at no. 2 bestows female profit, no. 3 gives wealth & no. 4 gives state pleasure which are good gains. Therefore, the main doors should be made in the East direction.

The South direction does not give any good result, so no door be made there.

In the West direction the main door should be built as it gives good results because of no 20 Pushpdant which gives profit of wealth.

In the North no 27 Mukhaya gives son and wealth, so it is good for family, if main door is made here. Beside this no 28 Bhallat gives Lakshmi and no 29 Som gives religious belief & modesty. It is also a good place for main door.

There are many views and ideas about the place for main door.

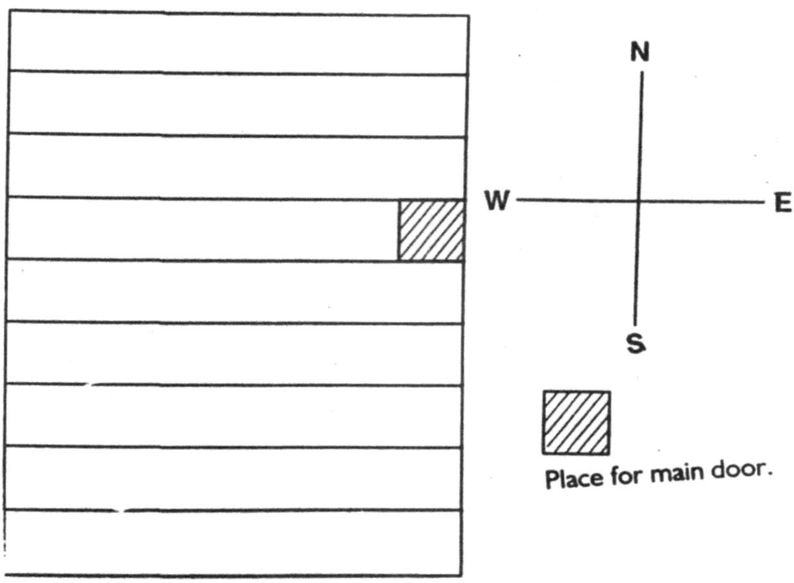

Navbhagam greham kurpat panchbhagam tu dakhsne.
Tribhagamuttre kritva shesh dwar prakalpayet.

In this method, the length of house (the length of direction in which the door is to be made) should be divided into 9 parts, among which 5 parts should be left in the right side and 3 parts in the left side and door should be made in last part, left therefore.

The right side of the house is the right part of the man while coming out of the house. The left side of the house is the left part of the man while coming out of house. If we are standing facing East then our right part is in the South direction; and our left part is in the North direction. Just like that only if the face of the house is in the East direction then the right part is in the South direction and the left part in the North direction.

That is to say that our right hand is towards the left hand of theirs and their right hand is towards our left hand.

According to this the man entering the house has the left part in the right side of the house and the right part in the left part of the house.

According to the Vaastu shastra there are four types of relation between the outer and the inner doors direction of the house. They are Utsang, Satya, Astatya and Prishtabhang.

(1) **Utsang** : When the outer and the inner door are in one direction facing each other is called Utsang. This is the best.

(2) **Satya** : When the outer main door is at the right side of inner door then is called Satya. This is also auspicious.

(3) **Apsatya** : When the outer door is at the left side of the inner door is called Apsatya which is not good.

(4) **Prishtabhang** : When the outer door is at the opposite direction of the inner door is called Prishtbhang which is also not good.

It has been seen that the main door should be best built in its specific place, and the doors should not be facing each other. There should be no door made in the middle of the breadth of the Hall. Door should not be made above another door. Main door should not be more thick or thin and door of the gate should be an automatic gate.

Main door mostly should be in the ratio of 1:2 i.e. the length should be double of breadth and not more or less than the ratio 1:2.

The minimum width should be of four feet. There should be no sound while closing & opening the door. The wood should be new for the main gate. One should not use the building material of the old house while making a new house. It does not give happiness.

The door-frame of the gate should be equal and it should be made at the equal angle. The door frame of the main gate should be ornamented with"Mangal kalash" and the main door should be more ornamented than the inner doors of the house.

The main gate should be always of two doors. If all the doors of house are of one door then also the main gate should be of two door & should open from inside.

DOOR VEDH

While making main gate it should be seen that there should be no door Vedh. If a main gate has any obstacle then it is called Door-Vedh. For example, If the main gate has pole, stairs, pathway, angle, big trees, thorny shrubs, machine or well in front then it has Door Vedh. These all should not be in front of the door and if it is at the double distance from the door, it is not harmful.

According to Vaastu shastra

If the main gate is in front of the way it is harmful for the Landlord. If the main gate has big trees in front of it, it is harmful for the children.

The road, in front of the main gate, has mud always, then it is mournful for the family, the door which has continous flow of water in front of it, then it wastes the money. If the main gate has a well in front of it, then the people suffer from Epilepsy. If it has temple then the house gets many harmful results. But if the house has any such ved thing at double the distance of the height of house or if a highway is between the house & the Vedh thing; then there is no Vedh fault.

If these things are at the back of the palace or simple house and also at the side of the house then there is no Vedh fault. The Vedh fault is there only when these things are in front of the main gate of the house.

Main Door

Besides Shahi door, Sadar door and Singh door is a Main door in a house from which we enter into the house. This door is also important like the main gate. The main gate has some principles as following.

(1) The main door at the N.Ishan is of best type. It helps the Landlord in many ways. If the main door is in the North Ishan and the heavy furnitures are kept in the South and West side of the room; and light weight articles in the North and South West. This is the basic principle of the building construction.

(2) East Ishan-The main door in this direction is also of best quality and the people residing in such type of houses are very brilliant intelligent and are wise scholars. The heavy articles are kept at the south of the room so that the way of going in & out is in the North direction.

(3) East Agnaya main door is of lowest category which gives very bad results.

(4) South Agnaya main door is of good quality which gives fruitful results. In this the furniture and the heavy articles are kept in west side of the room so that passage of going out & coming in are in the East directions; which gives good results.

(5) South Nairithya main door is of low quality which results in the loss of wealth, and the female of the house is always ill.

(6) West Nairithya main door is of low category which results in money-loss and the position of the head of house slides down.

(7) West Wayava main door is of high quality which is of very good omen, nature and is very lucky.

(8) North Wayava main door is of low category. The people residing here are of fickle minded, restless and unsteady.

Principles

(1) If the main door of the house is in the West then there should be a door in the East-side. Same way, if a main door is in the South, then one should be in the North side. This principle is important in all family houses. The movement of the people in this house is in the East face & North face.

(2) In a family quarter the doors and the windows can be made in all the four sides of the rooms but they should be in high quality areas, ie. The Vaastu shastra views should be kept in mind.

(3) While making doors in the house it should be kept in mind that the door-frame should not touch the main wall and the distance between the wall and the door frame should be of minimum 4 inches.

(4) The door, windows and the Almirahs of the house should face each other.

(5) If the main gate of the house is in the East direction, then the entrance door of the house should be in the East. This should be kept in mind that the entrance door should be made at the middle of the North side of the room so that the main gate falls in most effective position which is good for the welfare of the family residing there.

(6) If the main gate of the house is in the North direction then the entrance door should be in the North side at the middle of the East direction of the room.

(7) If the main gate of the house is at the West direction the entrance door of the house should be at the West direction of rooms. It should be in such a way that it should be in middle part of the room which augurs well for the main gate and will also increase the wealth.

(8) If the main gate of the house is in the South direction then the entrance door of the house should be at the room made in the South direction in such a way that it should be at the middle of the room. This sitiuation is suitable and useful for the family.

(9) If the door is made in lowest category place of the house then the family becomes the victim of disorders or deformities.

Number of Doors

The number of doors depends upon financial status of the landlord and also upon his circumstances. As the unwanted doors are harmful for the house, likewise the doors which are needed but are not made are harmful to the family. Therefore, we will dicuss these aspects serially.

One door—

In any house if only one door is made, it is due to poverty only. If one door is made, then the same should be made only in an East and North direction of the house. Then only it will be suitable. The house facing South & West direction should not have one door. Inside the house, the one door can be in the Nairithya and Ishan rooms.

Two Doors—

If two doors are to be made in the house, then it should be in the East and South or East and West or in the East and North direction.

But never in the South and West. It can be in the South and North or South or East. Same way two doors can be in the West and North or North and East.

In house where the rooms are in Nairithya or Ishan Angle can have two doors built. In the Nairithya room the doors are in the North or East Ishan direction.

Three Doors—

If three doors are made in a house then the East side should not be left. Leaving the South part the door made in the North, East and West is best. In the three door house if they are made in North, East and South leaving the West part is good. Leaving the North part is not a good sign. In any case the Nairithya room should not have the three doors.

Four Doors—

If the right direction according to the compass is all right, then the doors can be made in all the four directions. But even then there should not be four doors in the Nairithya rooms.

Boundary Wall & Main Gate

Boundary wall is very important for whole family of the house and industries.

The boundary wall not only saves the house there but it saves the house and the industries from the harmful results of the Vaastu. From every point of view boundary wall is essential.

This had been written before that only the breadth of South and West part of the boundary wall should be thicker than the East and North part. Beside this, there are certain principles attributed to the main door.

(1) If the house is East-faced and the entrance door is in front of the boundary wall, then it is of best quality. It is more effective when the boundary wall is made at North left place of house, and a door is made at Ishan (East of the boundary wall) ana without this door, the door made earlier will be of low category.

(2) In the South faced house a main gate is made at the front of the place left in the East, in the South Agnaya angle. If a main gate is already made in the boundary, in front of entrance

door of the house, then also the second door is neccessary which will give precedence to the first door.

(3) In the West-faced house the entrance door in the boundary is in front of the main door of house, then also a door should be made in West Wayava at the front of the place left in North of the house. Because with out it the first door is of low quality.

(4) In the North-faced house if the entrance-door is at the main gate in the boundary wall, then also a door is needed in North Ishan side which will get the first door in good category.

(5) If the main gate of house is made, at center of the extension of the boundary wall, then its face could be towards any direction. In this type the main gate made at the front of the entrance-door is free from any Vaastu fault. And there is no need to make a second door, even at the best site of the house.

(6) The best quality of door made in the boundary wall of house should always be utilised then only it will give good results.

(7) The sheds for the car should be at the Agnaya or Wayava direction of the house. Shed should be made at the distance from the compound of East and North wall and should be made close to the walls of the South or West side. The shed can be made at the Nairithya side also which is closer to the walls of South or West side.

(8) In the East and North faced house, the boundary wall be kept lower than the main gate in the East and North direction. In the West and the South-faced houses boundary wall can be kept low, high or even.

(9) If the boundary wall is cracked or broken in the South or West Nairithya or in East Aganya or North Wayava then it should be mended quickly which will save us from the harmful effects of the Vaastu.

Residential Plan

Till now we have studied about the house and the plots. Now we will discuss about the residential house. While making a residential house we have to keep in mind certain principles—

(1) **Land** : In the house construction the choice of Land is very essential. In the Vaastu shastra the experience has its own importance. After choosing the Vaastu-Land the things which have to be observed are suitable surroundings, open air, water processing. Apart from these many more points are kept in mind.

If the plot, purchased for house coustruction, is of square type, then it will give to the family peace and prosperity. If rectangular plot is purchased then it should be seen that the length should not be more than the double of the breadth of the Land.

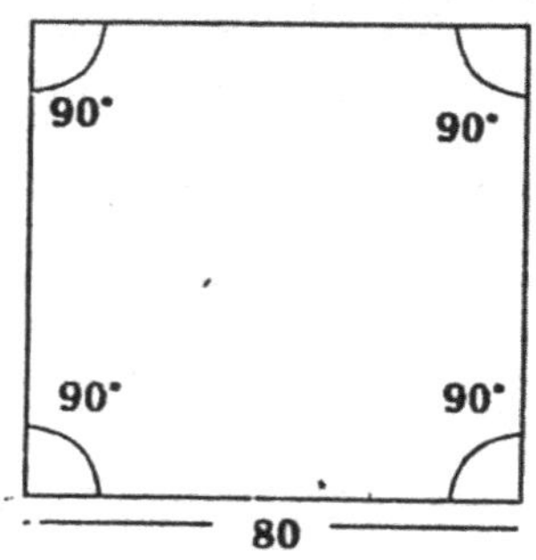

A plot in 80 feet square at –90° is the best plot.

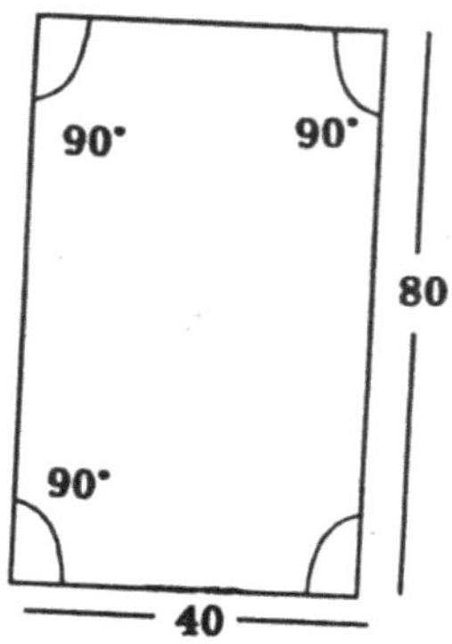

80 ft.rectangular plot at –90° will be the best plot.

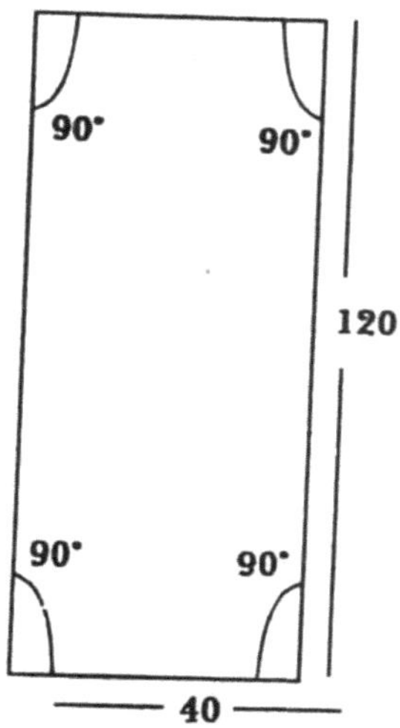

90° rectangular plot, with its length three times of its width will be a harmful plot.

Rectangular Plot

Such a plot is said to be lucky and this plot also provides wealth, health and prosperity. According to the figure the plot should have all the angles at 90°and the direction at the right position.

According to the direction, we have the way on which side of the plot, because while making the house we have to make the main-gate towards the pathway. The Gomukhi and Shermukhi plot should be avoided. The shermukhi plot is useless for residential purposes.

If the front part of the plot is broad and the back part is narrow then it is called Shermukhi. According to the Vaastu this plot is not suitable. The people residing here get ill due to air hunger.

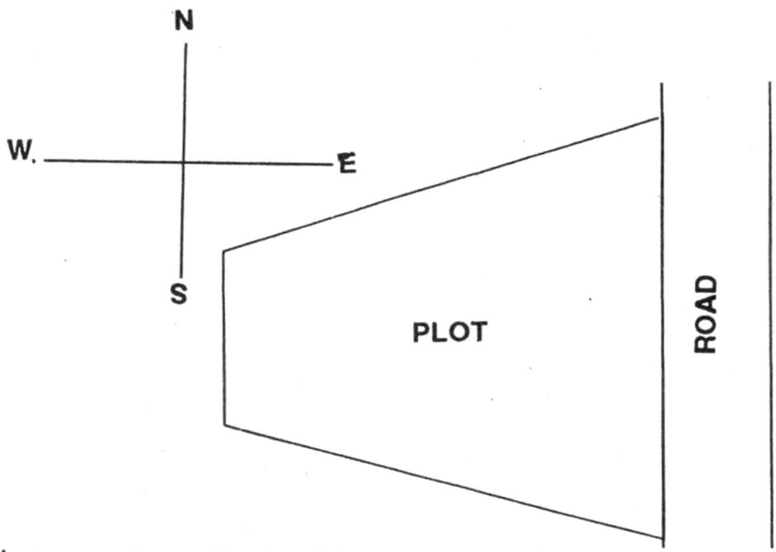

Just opposite to this plot if the front part of the plot is narrow and the back part is broad then this plot is called Gomukhi plot; this plot is also not good for the house construction according to the Vaastu concept. The people residing here become abnormal right from the birth. A child born on this plot is devoid of intelligence. This plot is not suitable for the house. The people who live here are narrow minded.

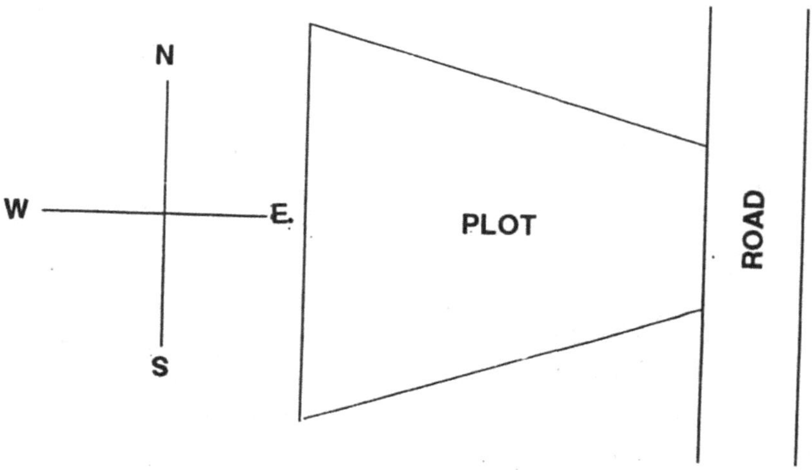

Thus it has been seen that the square & rectangular shape plots are best among all the shapes & sizes of the plot. The Nairithya angle should be 90° of the plot according to the Vaastu principle.

Soil

The soil of the plot should be solid. when the soil in middle of the plot is high or is sloped down the East or North East side of the plot then the people living there get full advantages of rays of Sun, falling on these places of the plot. The Vaastu land should be high in the South-west. The high-rise house from East to West, is Sun-Vedh. The people who live in these houses do not get ample amount of sunlight. The high-rise house, from North to South is chandravedhi.

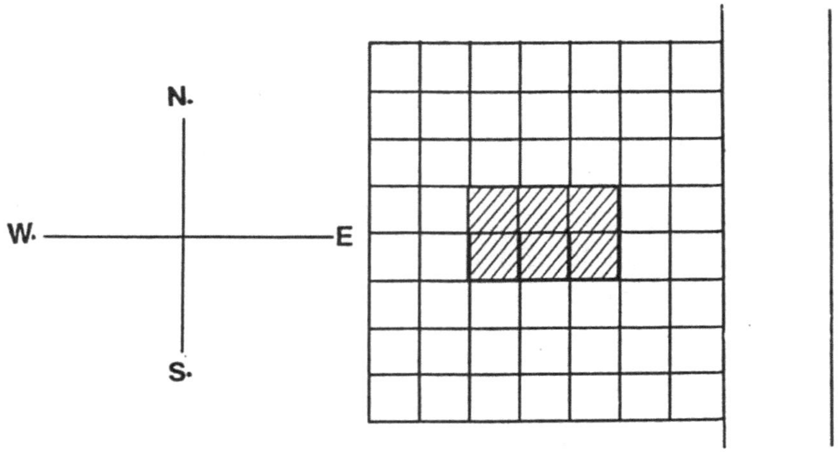

Plot suitable for construction— This construction is from the East to the West, and is Suryavedhi construction.

While making house you should leave ample open space inside the boundary wall on all the four sides. The house should be made in the South-West. The more open space should be left in the East and North. There should be open space for the "PARIKRAMA" inside the boundary wall around the house.

Plot suitable for construction—If the construction is towards the South from the North it is chrandravedhi construction. This is a good & lucky construction.

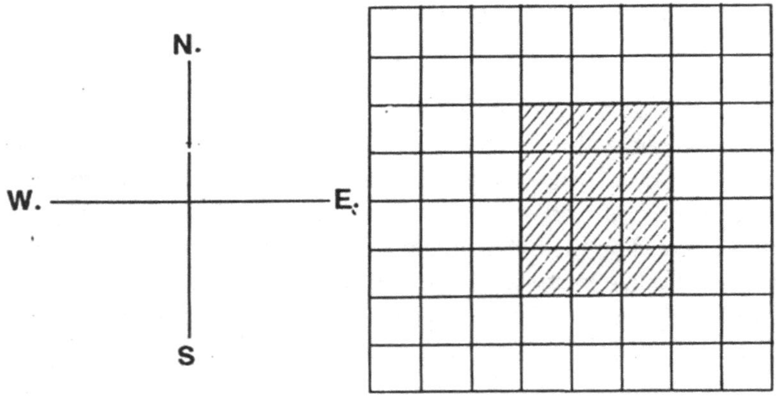

Water

After choosing the construction place, one should decide as to from which direction water is coming. If you use the well, Boring, Tubewell or municipality or corporation water or any other source of water then think about it carefully.

But the water processing place should be in the East or in Ishan side. Swimming pool should also be in the East or North side of the house. In the house the water supply should be from North or East. The water of the Bathroom should also be in East-North side. Thus the slope should be in North-East direction of the house; and the rain water should be let out from the North-East side.

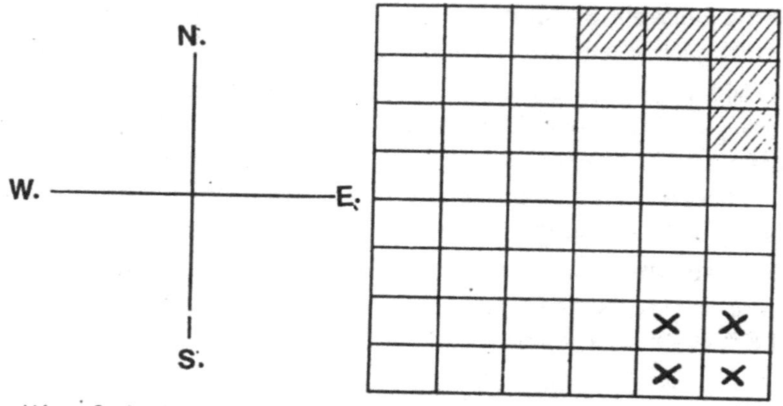

Water fcility should be in North-East or Ishan directions only.

Electricity Meter & Fusebox

Electricity is the part of fire. Among the main components of the energy Electricity is very important. Thus the wiring and meter and the power house should be in the Agni direction. This principle is also applicable for factories and business areas. The power house in the Agni direction minimises the fear of high and harmful results of the electricity. The main power house should never be in the Ishan, North, South and Nairithya direction.

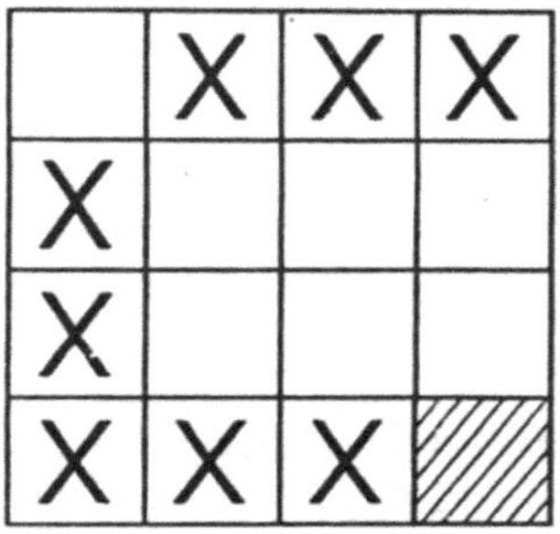

Suitable for use of power house.

X Not suitable.(never use such places for erecting power-houses)

Septic Tank

The septic tank is always made behind the toilet and the bathroom; as it is very heavy. Thus the best place for the septic tank is in the South. In the Agnaya side it is made in the Soutn direction. In the Nairithya there should be no septic tank made because any hole or making hole is bad in thc Vaastu shastra. No septic tank in the North East should be made.

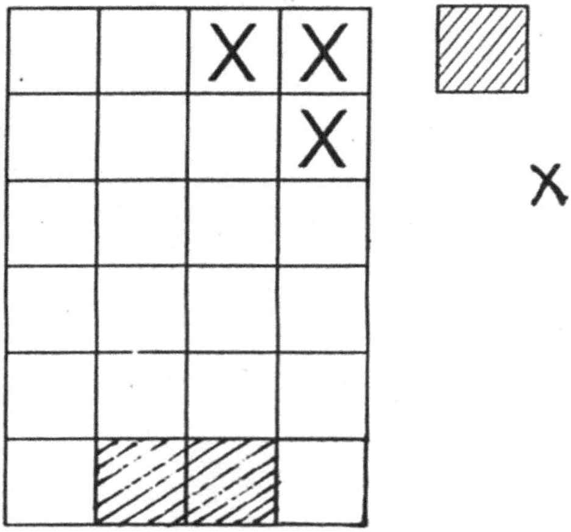

Suitable for septic tank construction.

Not suitable for the septic tank. It is very bad for the family members. The family will be separated & the business will be finished.

Clothes Washing

Till now I have seen, people often do not give attention to this room in the house. Even if the house has every facility even then they do not have room for the washing clothes even though washing clothes is very essential in the daily life. Specially in the rainy season the females have many problems in washing clothes as they do not have separate room for it.

In my opinion, there should be a separate room for the washing clothes. Whether the clothes are washed by hand or machines hot water is needed so the washing room should be in the Agni side, so that the water flows in the North-East.

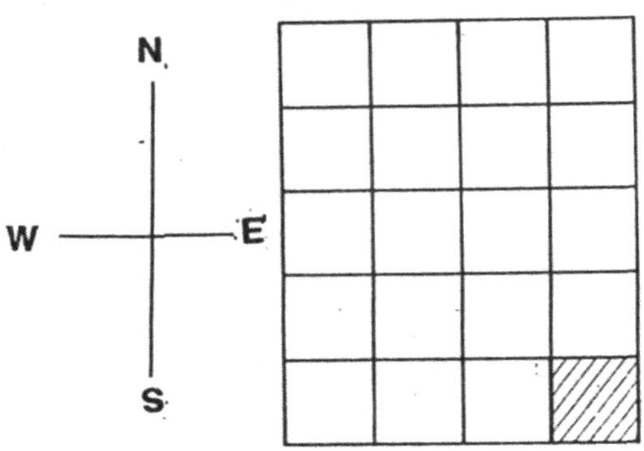

Place suitable for washing clothes.

Godown Room

To keep the useful things in a house there should be a Bhandar griha, godown in the factory and store room for the office. Actually there is no need to search for any thing from the godown room which saves time as all the things are kept safe. The godown room should be always in the Wayava. If machinery is kept there then there will be no theft and there will be no problems of rats in store room full of grains.

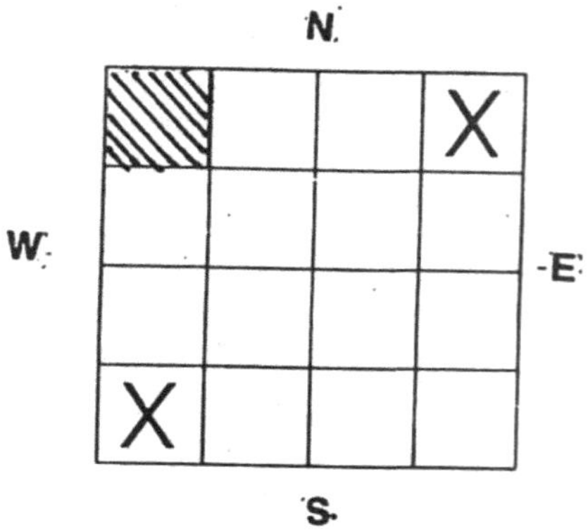

Suitable for godown room.

X

Not suitable for godown room but if made, the landlord faces many problems.

Machines in factory

The heavy machines in the factory are kept in the South as far as possible. After that in the West side can be kept. No heavy things should be kept in the Ishan and North side; these sides should not be over loaded as far as possible.

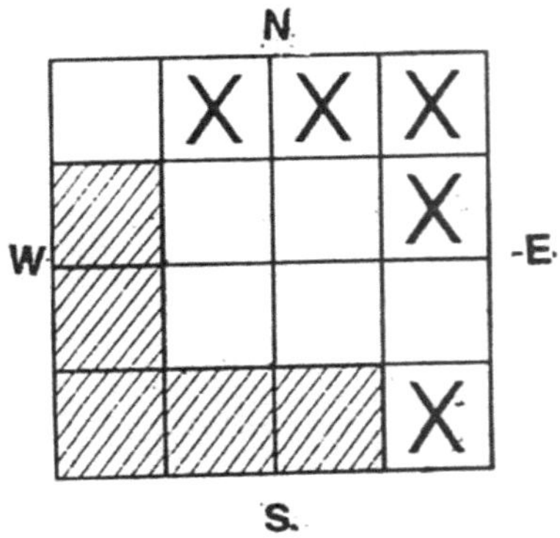

These places can be used for keeping heavy things. In house safes, almirahs are kept and in the factory heavy machines can be kept here.

These places should be kept light, because they will be best for the factory.

Kitchen

This is a very emotional place in the house. The health of each member of the house depends upon this room, specially of the stomach and the heart. I have seen the people and the Landlord suffering from stomach problem and heart diseases if the kitchen is made in a wrong place.

While making food, fire is needed in huge amount so the Kitchen should be in the Agni angle i.e. South East direction. If you use gas or stove or wood for making food, then these should be kept in South of the kitchen and the face of the person preparing food should be in the East always. While using the direction in this way the house lady who prepares food is always healthy and the foods are tasty.

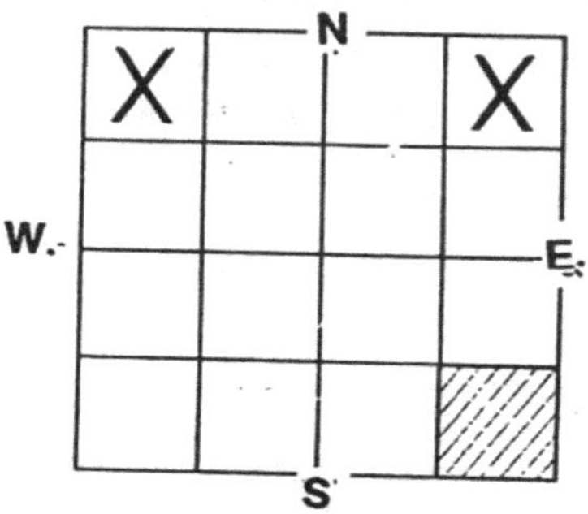

[hatched square] Kitchen in this place is suitable and saves gas and fuels. Foods prepared are tasty & healthy.

X Kitchen made in these places results into heart and stomach problems.

Ventilation, Windows, Verandah & Balcony

These four things are very essential for any house; These are made in the house for the movement of air. Thus as far as possible these four things should be made in Wayava, the direction of air. By doing so the people living here will be healthy.

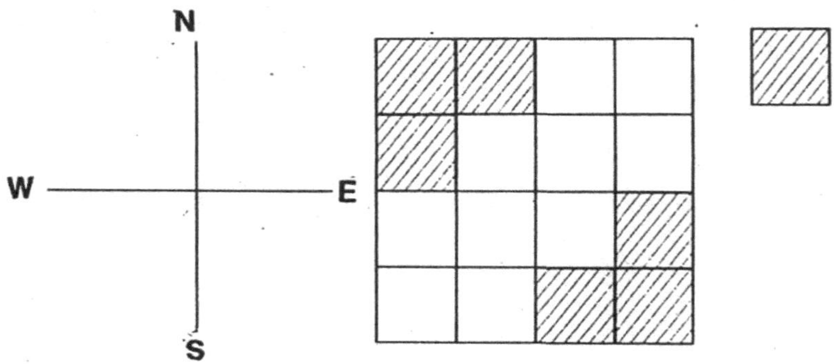

The whole construction should be more airy. More air means better health and wealth

Worship-Room

The worship room should be in the Ishan, North or East direction and face of the God in the South or West so that, while worshiping we face towards the East and North. This will add to prosperity in the family. The worship room should be made separate which is very essential. It should not be in sleeping room. For worship room, Ishan is the best place, after that comes North and East. Apply these directions in use so the Gods live in the house & no ill befalls on the family living here.

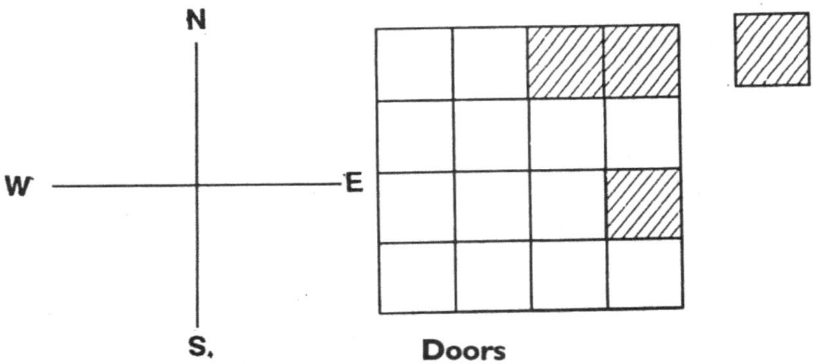

Doors

About the doors we have discussed before very briefly. Thus, the doors made in accordance with God are of best category. As the nerves hold the main power in the body, similarly the door is important to the house. So while making doors, safety is ensured.

Main Bed Room

The landlord's main bed room should be in the South West. The bed should be attached with the walls of South or West so that more empty space is left in North-East. Bedroom should not be in Ishan or Agnaya direction. The bedroom made in the Wayava gives mental problems. The people sleeping there do not enjoy sound sleep. In a house if there are two bedroom then one should be in the South West and the other should be in the North-West direction.

Bedroom in the East gives bad health while in the South gives better health. West side bedroom is good while the North bedroom is bad. While sleeping the head should be in the South and the leg in North direction. The head of the Man is North pole & the leg is South pole. This does not interfere with the entrance of Magnetic waves, which keep the brain of the sleeping people normal and well poised.

If these facilities are not possible then the bed can be kept along the West wall and the head of the man in the East. But never in the North direction.

Sleep refreshes men. Thus the sleep should be peaceful and carefree. Following the Vaastu principles you can enjoy sound sleep whole life.

The steel almirah or the heavy things should be in the South or West or South West along the wall of South & West and the the face of the almirah in the North or East. The Valuable things can be kept there.

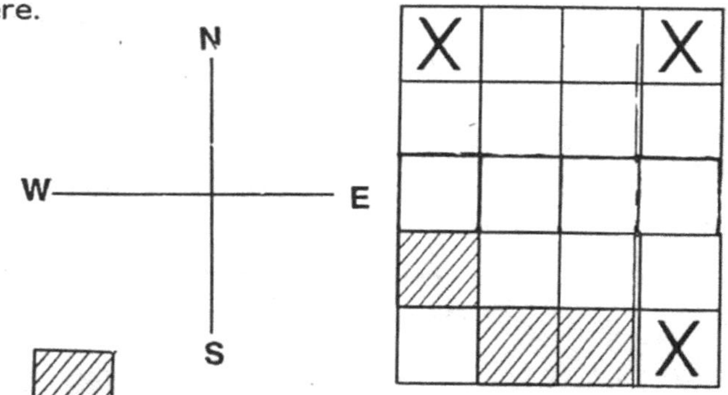

Best suitable place for bedrooms.

X Not suitable for bedrooms, makes bad sleep and restless sleep to the Landlord.

Bath Room

The great importance of bathroom we can see in our old holy books. In the Mughal period also it enjoyed a respectful position. The bathing sports is very good which takes away all the mental tensions. The Bathroom has its own importance.

But now people are making the bathroom day-by-day smaller and smaller and not giving much attention to its construction. But in my opinion the bathroom should have the same importance as the bedroom.

Remember this that the kitchen and the bathroom reflect your good & healthy mental position. It keeps you both healthy & peaceful.

Simply now-a-days three types of bathroom can be seen—

(1) Bathroom attached with bedroom of the house.

(2) Bathroom common for everyone in the house.

(3) Outside the house but attached with the house.

According to the Vaastu the common bathroom can be made in the North or East direction. Now-a-days toilets are made attached with the bathrooms. The toilet seats should be kept in such a way that the man, sitting thereon, should face the South, West or North but never the East side.

Some Vaastu shastris do not think even West direction to be good because the Sun sets in the West and that is an insult to the Sun God.

Toilets should not be in the Ishan angle, it is harmful. If made in the Nairithya angle then no hole should be dug. The toilet-seat should be made on the platform; and the septic tank should be in the middle of North & East.

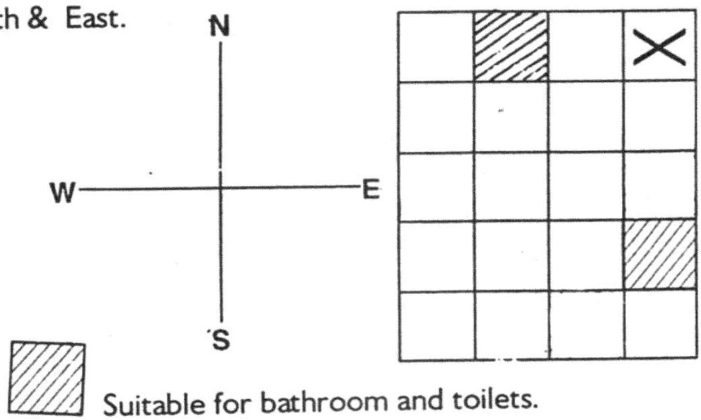

Suitable for bathroom and toilets.

X Not suitable.

Guest House

In the house the guest room should be in the North or West. The bathroom inside this room should also be conforming to the above factors. Wayava direction is also good for guest room.

Guest room made in these directions keep the guest happy and peaceful with you.

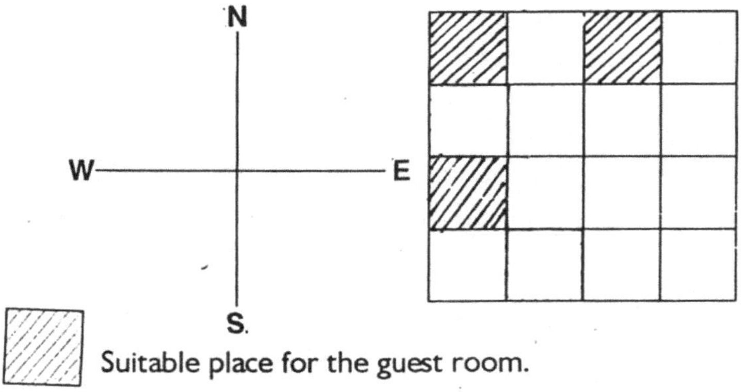

Suitable place for the guest room.

Sitting or Drawing Room

Drawing room is said to be the heart of any house. The whole glamour and the decoration can be seen in the drawing room itself. So, main attention should be given to the drawing room while constructing a house. The people like friends, business people or relatives who come to meet you sit in this room only. Thus drawing room is important from the point of Vaastu also. The drawing room becomes more attractive as it is bigger than the other rooms. The most important room of the house is made the drawing room. It should be in the South or West. Hence this room is decorated with the costly things—Sofa, Almirah etc are kept along the wall of South and West, keeping the North and the East side more empty.

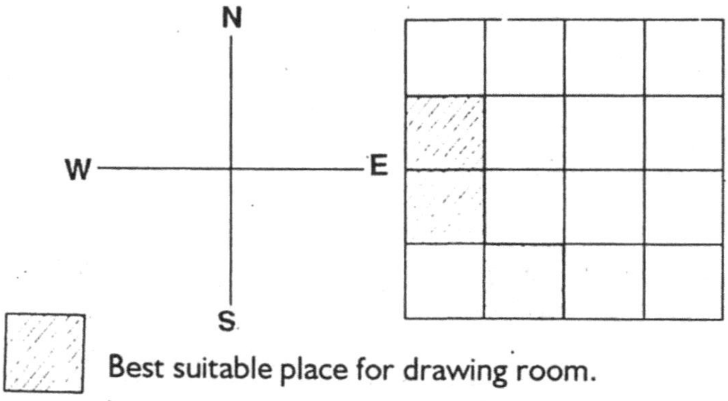

Best suitable place for drawing room.

Study Room

The study room should be in the North East of the house, but this is the place for the worship room. Vaastu shastra maintains and places the study room at par with the Worship Room, according it equal importance.

Besides this Nairithya angle is also suitable for study room. The child studying with the face towards the East gets more intelligence and stays stable. Face is blossomed with beauty and innocence.

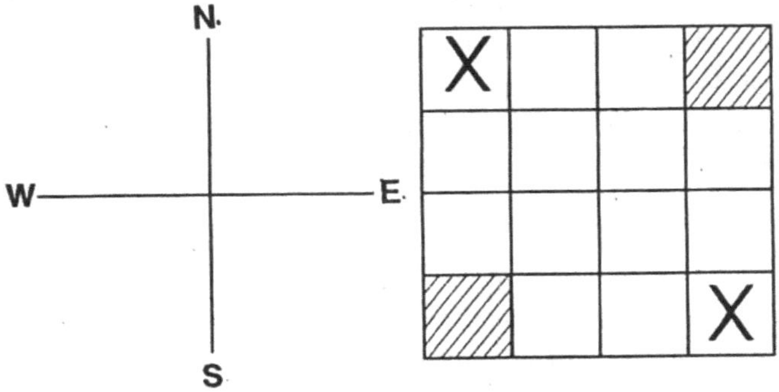

 Suitable for study room.

X Not suitable for study room. Child's mind gets restless and deviates from his studies.

Entertainment or Musical Room

Music is a form of sweet sound. Air is its medium. For music ample amount of air is needed. Air keeps control over the sargam of music. Actually the origin of up and down of sargams of the music depends upon the air only. Thus this room should be in the Wayava direction.

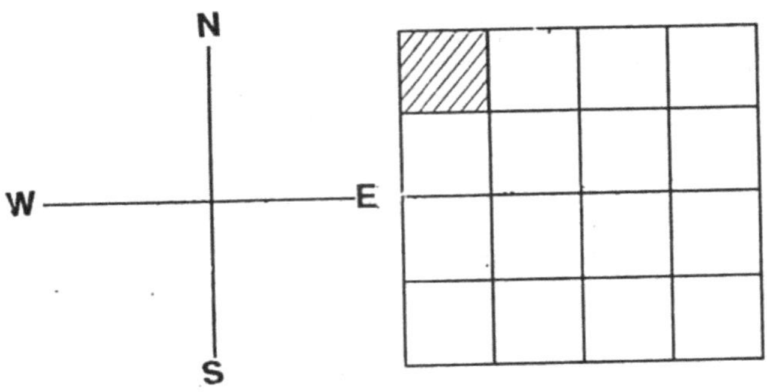

 Best suitable place for the music room.

Servants Quartar

In the Agnaya or Wayava angle the servant quarter should be made along the walls of South East, North & West leaving at least 3 1/2 ft distance. House should not be made attached with wall. As far as possible weight should not be put on the walls of the North and East.

Water Tank

The water tank can be built above the South West or North West of the house; but not above the Ishan angle. In the Ishan angle underground water tank can be made. Keep in mind that the Nairithya angle should be the highest in the house; If by keeping the water tank it becomes low then the wall of the Nairithya angle should be lifted higher.

Stairs

The stairs directions should be in the right direction of the watch needles. The stairs number should be always odd & uneven. ie. 5, 11, 17, 23, i.e. While dividing it by 3, it will give two in the last. Leaving the Ishan angle we can make stairs in any direction.

In the North and East of the house shrubs & herbs can be grown. These shrubs should not be thorny. The sweet and beautiful trees should be there. Big trees should be not near the house; the roots of these trees will make the base of the house weak & it will produce insects and worms.

Ways to Remove faults in the Modern house

The house in which you are living is not according to the Vaastu principle then you can make it proper with some correction then it will be fruitful. like making the height of the house right by the T.V. antenna. The water processing fault can be removed with the help of water pipe line. By keeping the heavy material in the South the house can be made according to the Vaastu.

Outer Room : Keeping in mind the different works the outer rooms are made away from the main house for servants, stores or for guests or for entertainment. These rooms are made with walls of the South or West boundary wall but never along the wall of North or East boundary wall.

The doors of these rooms should be in the North or East according to your necessity.

Correction of faults by Out house

(1) If the expanse of the plot is from North to South and the

house constructed in the North part & the South part is kept empty then the family can be protected from the harmful results of the Vaastu when the outhouse is built in the Nairithya angle having the floor of the outhouse higher than the main house floor; and no door should be in the West and South of the outhouse.

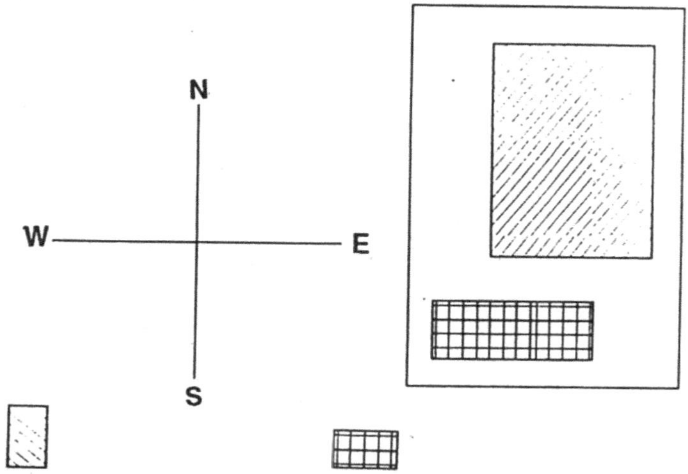

Main construction place *Out house construction.*

(2) If the vastness of the plot is from West to East and the house is built in the East leaving the west part empty then in that plot outhouse is very essential to be built in the Nairithya side. The floor of the outhouse should be higher than that of the main house and there should be no door in the South.

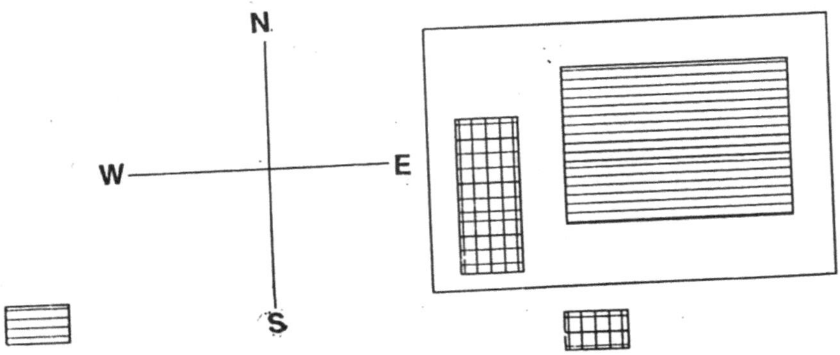

The house construction. *Constructed Outhouse.*

(3) In the North part if a house is built along the boundary wall of the North part and vacant place left in the South, then some part of North should be dismantled down, and an outhouse should be built alongwith the South boundary-wall. If there is no vacant place in the East, then the Ishan-built place should be pulled down; because without this the outhouse, built in the Nairithya would be fruitless. There should be no door built in South boundary wall. If a door is built there, then it should be closed. There should be no empty place in the West part of the out house.

Group Housing and Vaastu Law

Till now we have studied about the construction of houses, their plans and Vaastu. In these houses there is only one landlord who makes the house according to his Vaastu choice. In this he keeps the Vaastu law in his mind and makes the house according to his necessity and comfort.

But now a days in Metropolis, small and medium towns, due to complex and tough competition for single house is becoming day-by-day very tough. So the government and private concerns have started making group houses like apartments. In this group housing planning many houses are with Vaastu faults and many without any fault. Therefore, while dividing these plots for making houses if the Laws of Vaastu is seen and used then they can build with less Vaastu fault. These buildings should be made very carefully.

(1) The colony should be designed in such a way that every plot stands evenly from North to the South direction.

(2) There should be empty place all around the colony.

(3) Try to keep the maximum number of plots facing towards the East or North.

(4) The maximum open space should be in the North and less open space in the Southern part.

(5) The land should be purified according to your necessity.
(6) Land should be more open from East To West.
(7) The underground water facility for the whole house should be in the North East part.
(8) The maximum height of the colony should be in the South and West.
(9) If the water tank is possible to make on the terrace, then it should be in the South-West direction.
(10) The height of colony should be low in the North and East.
(11) To keep the colony green the garden should be in the North, East or North-East.
(12) Verandah in the North and East.
(13) The transformer and other electricity materials should be in the South East.
(14) Windows should be in the East and North mainly.
(15) The gap between the plots should be according to the law of Vaastu, the breadth comparable to the height of the building.
(16) Windows should not be in the South and West part.
(17) In the colony, while making houses on the plot, more open spaces should be around the houses and much more open space in the North & East.
(18) Plots may be adjacent to each other but walls of houses should not touch.
(19) Every house of the colony should have very strong wall in West & South part.
(20) The light walls of the houses of the colony in the North and East.
(21) More doors in East and North and less doors in the West and South.
(22) The flow of water out-let should be in the Ishan, North or East direction.
(23) Septic tank in the middle East or middle North.
(24) The boundary wall should be thick and high in the South and West; thin and low boundary walls in the North and East part.
(25) If the main pathway is possible, then the gate should be in the North-East.
(26) The gate of the house should be in the South or South East of the house facing the South direction.

(27) The door of the house facing West should be in the West or North-West but never in the South-West.

(28) The bedroom should be in the South West of each house.

(29) Kitchen should be made in the South-East.

(30) The only room in the North East should be the worshiproom.

(31) Bathroom should be in the South part.

(32) The doors and windows should be even & plain.

(33) The level of the Verandah should be low than that of main house floor.

(34) No Verandah in the West & South be made.

(35) Corridor should be in the North-East.

(36) The roof of the corridor should be like the Verandah or lower than the Verandah level.

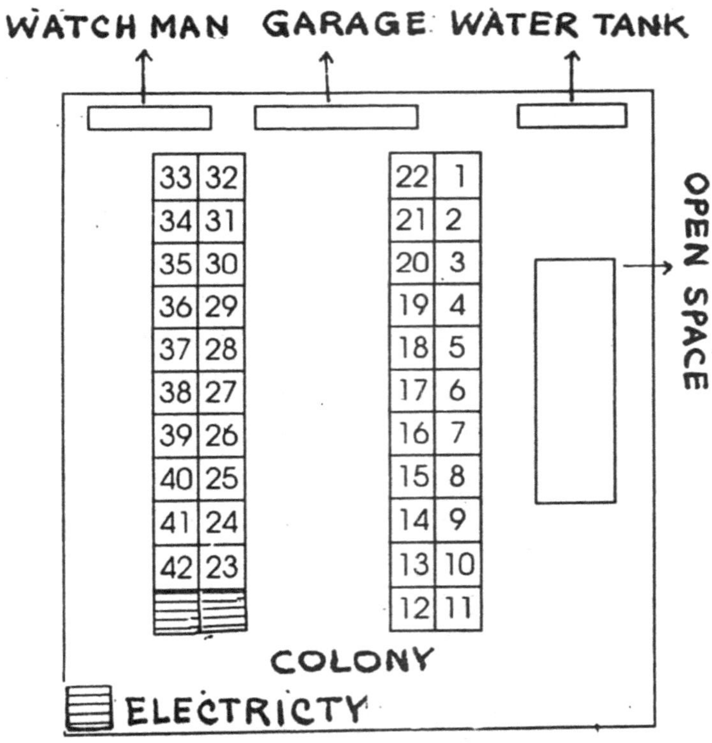

(37) The stairs being fortified should be in the South West.

(38) If a house is neccessary to be built for the night gaurd, then it should be lower than the height of the main houses and should

be in the South-East or North-West. Alongwith the night gaurd house the colony garrage can be built here.

A diagram is given below to show in a colony the houses according to the Vaastu are best, good and faulty.

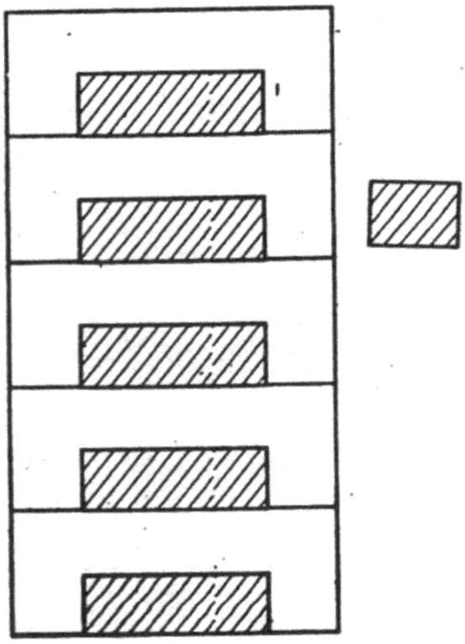

This construction is of best quality. In this the one wall of the boundary wall is utilised for the construction, which is very best for the Vaastu house.

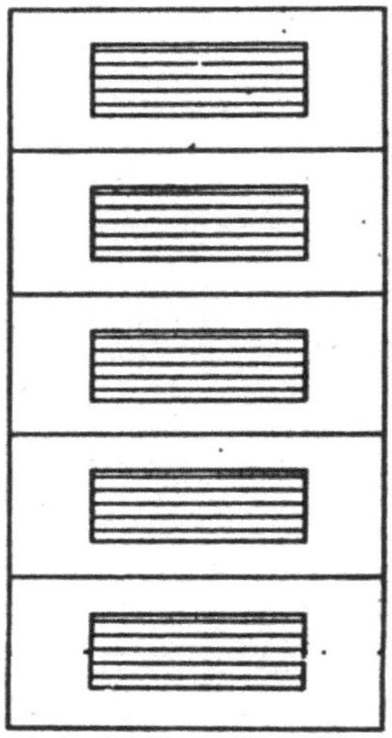

This construction falls under good category. Every house is built separately. Boundary wall is not taken into account for the building of house.

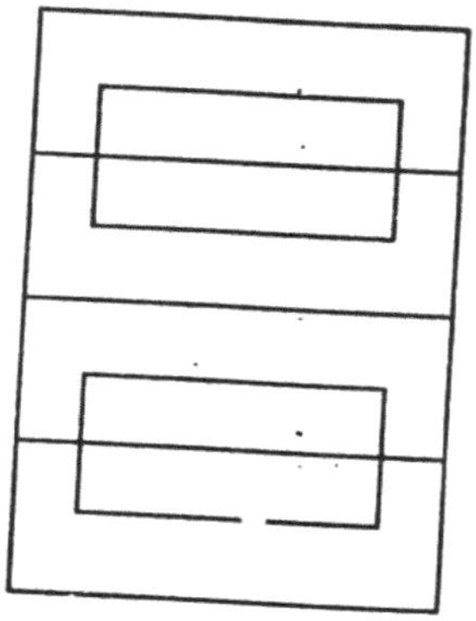

This construction is with Vaastu fault which should be better avoided. In this two flats are built jointly which is a construction related fault.

Multistoried Building

Due to economic profit, scarcity of land, heavy increase in population and modification of towns, big builders and businessmen are turning towards the multistory buildings or complex construction. With the construction of buildings the main aspects to look for is the land, soil and direction.

The best category of land is towards the East and North facing pathways; then making of the Vaastu building on this plot is very simple and easy. Then also it is clear that not every aspect of Vaastu will be incorporated in this building. Then also we have to purify the land and maintain the Vastu law, then we can live happily.

(1) The Vaastu principle for the land is applicable everywhere and anywhere in same way. Therefore the land has to be chosen very carefully.

(2) According to the law the height of first floor should be less than the ground floor height by 1\12 part. But this law is in practice upto 5-6 floor building and that also only in the multi storied building.

(3) The building should be constructed, leaving open space all around it. More open space in the North & East and less in the South & West.

(4) The entrance door in the East or North as far as possible.

(5) For the multistoried building rectangular equl-angled land is

much preferred. The people residing in this place get common facility and happiness.

(6) While making multistory building or, big hotels or huge Cinema hall one has to leave lots of open space in the front part. Two gates should be made : entrance gate & main gate. More open space in the East & North sides & less in the South & West sides.

(7) Car parking is very essential in these huge buildings. So the car parking space & the lawn should be made in the Ishan portion.

(8) The slope of the plot should be in the North East.

(9) The flats as far as possible should be in the East and North side.

(10) The multistory buildings are made very high & huge. So, one should keep in mind that the peaple who are residing in the lower portion should get ample amount of light, sun rays and air.

(11) The lower flats should be higher than the upper flats in the multistory buildings.

(12) The stairs should be near the lifts which should be clockwise, like the needle of a clock, and should not stand erect.

(13) Water tank should be in the Ishan angle.

(14) In one building there should be three water wells bored to the different depths because in summer season the water level goes down & water crisis arises.

(15) The Nairithya angle should be in high altitude.

(16) To avoid sound pollution, one should not give flats to the people who deal in iron sheets, rods or angles. Sound and vibration makes the building foundation weak and thus provides problems to the people residing there as sound passes very easily from one flat to another in such buildings.

(17) The waste water drainage should be through underground channel.

(18) Every flat should have more windows and Ventilation.

(19) If there is a hotel in a building then the kitchen should be in the Agnaya angle otherwise people in the flats will face problem of gas and smoke.

(20) It is neccessary to see that the flats from the ground floor to top should have gradual tapering of height. If the first floor is

11ft, then the second floor should be of 10\1\2 ft & the 3rd floor is of 10ft. so on and so forth. In this way the gravity of earth & the grip on building would be balanced.

In this way we see that many safety laws are observed while making multistoryed building.

I am giving an example of a building in Raipur which is made in an East facing plot and is very popular.

RISHABH COMPLEX

M.G. ROAD, RAIPUR (M.P.)

GROUND FLOOR PLAN

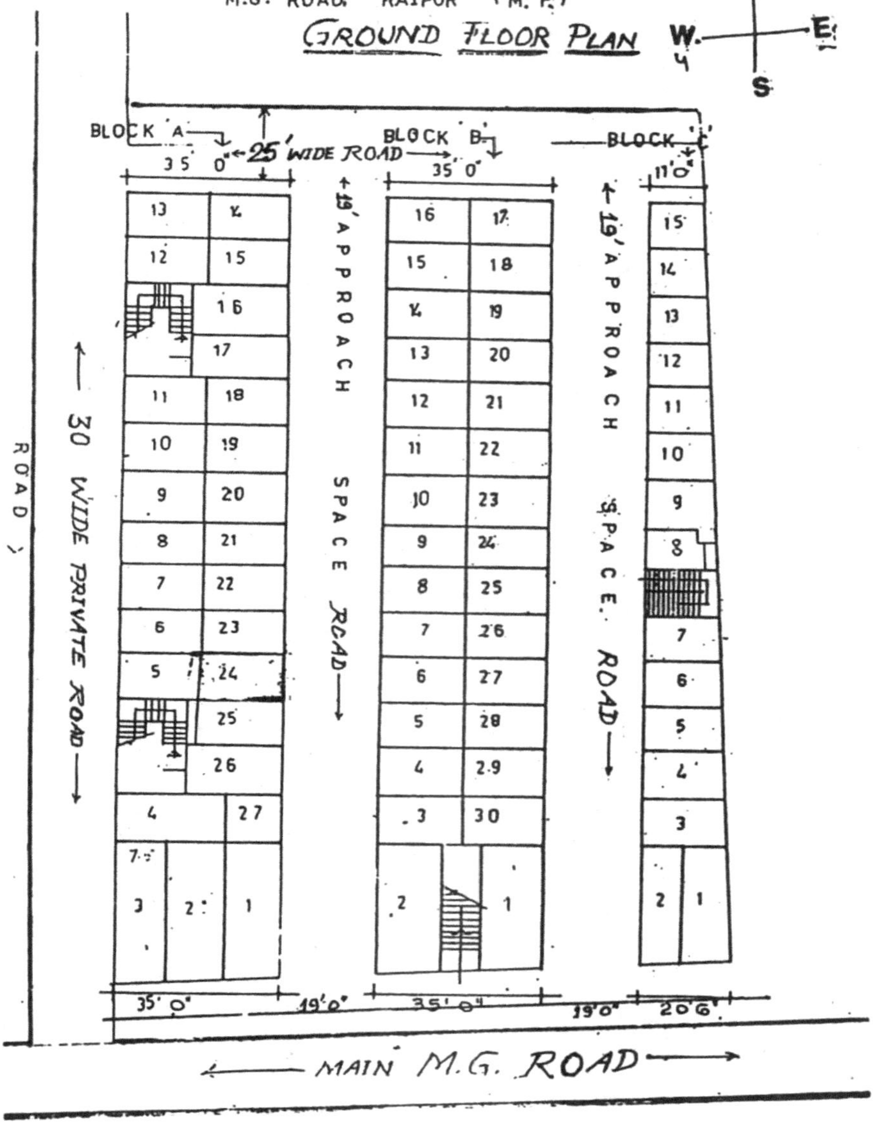

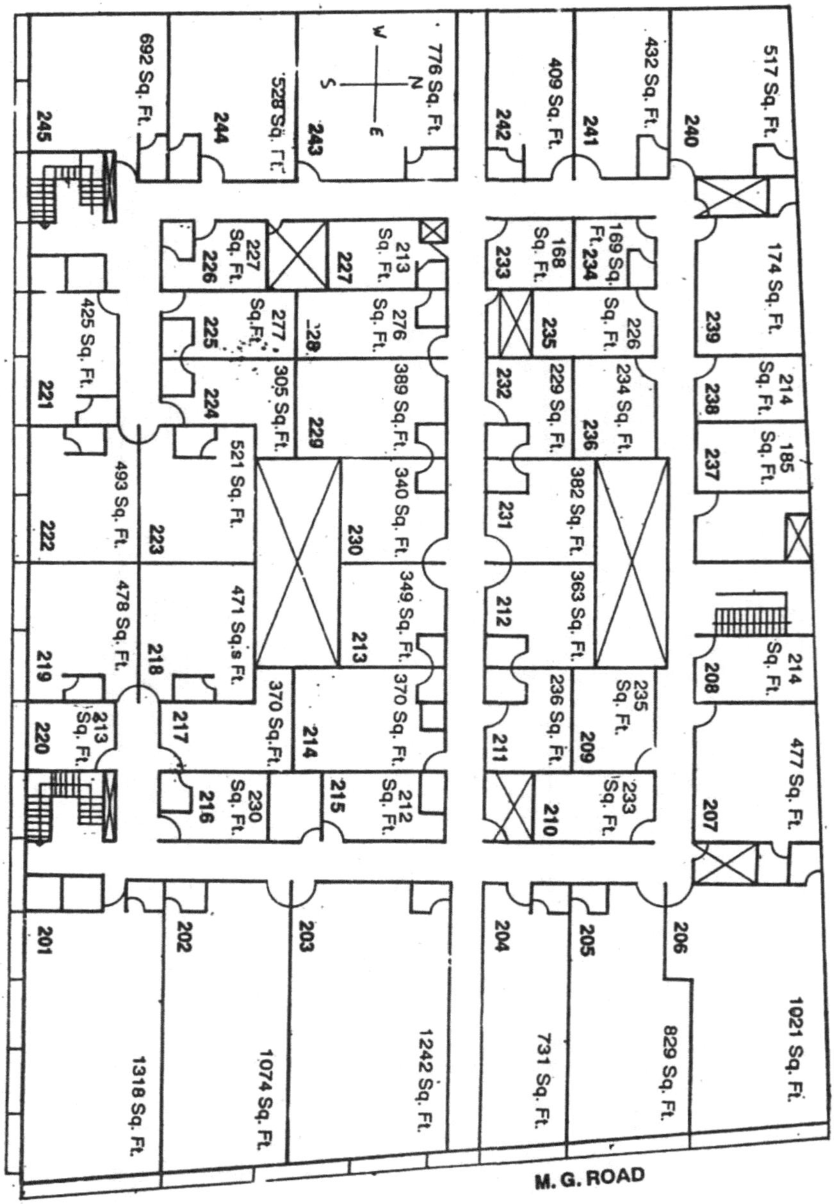

SECOND & THIRD FLOOR PLANE OF RISHABH COMPLEX AT. M.G. ROAD, RAIPUR (M.P.)

RISHABH COMPLEX, M.G. ROAD, RAIPUR

Commercial Complexes

As people living in a Vaastu house are happy and prosperous like businessmen in a Vaastu commercial complex get fame and wealth and their business runs peacefully. People doing business in a non-Vaastu complex face many types of problems and I have seen, in the end, that these business places get closed.

Thus while establishing any business like—Office, Showroom, Restaurant, Bar, Mill, Factory etc. one has to have some knowledge of Vaastu before investing lakhs of money on it; because it should give profit.

First of all one has to choose a plot very safely after seeing all the area around for the business; because the whole business depends upon the choice of plot; in which the direction is an essential point. If the direction of the face of showroom or office is in East then it is of best quality. This direction will always give profit to the business people. The East direction is the place of rising sun which is in motion till the sunset & which is indicative of progress & intelligence and wealth direction.

If the plot is of West facing, then the businessman faces sometime tough competition and low profit in the business but this plot is also said to be good.

After East, comes North faced plot. The business on this plot rises and gives prosperity to the man. The business becomes very popular and the person gets lakhs of rupees in one generation only. It is said that North faced plot is very favourable and lucky for the landlord and coming generation, This landlord makes three more complexes in the future from this business by earning on the North faced plot.

Business is not good in the South faced plot. The people loose their own money also and the business goes declining gradually and never get any success throughout life.

These laws of Vaastu shastra has been seen to be true. But sometimes changing little bit of the angle and sitting arrangement and the decoration of inside the office, the people get the profit of North facing plot on this plot. But these plots should be square or rectangle in shape.

In big cities and metropolis many complexes are made on the square or reactangle plots on which the showrooms and offices are made in every direction. Some times the plots are of triangular, semi circular or of any other shape and no great attention is given to the direction. Then also the businessmen should make the counter and sitting place according to the Vaastu even when the plot direction is somewhat wrong. The business men should sit facing East and North.

Some examples of plot and their results

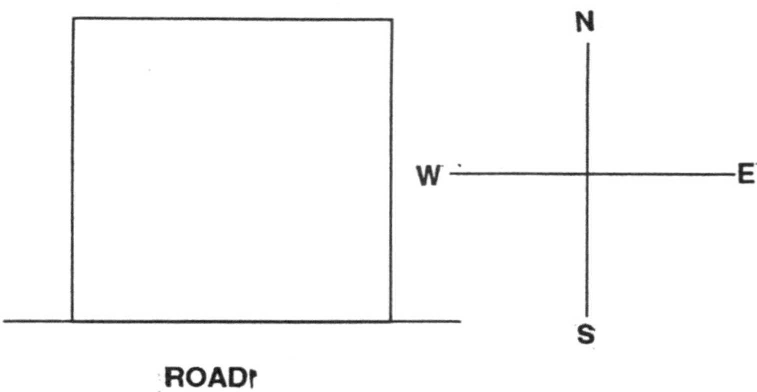

This is square & of best quality.

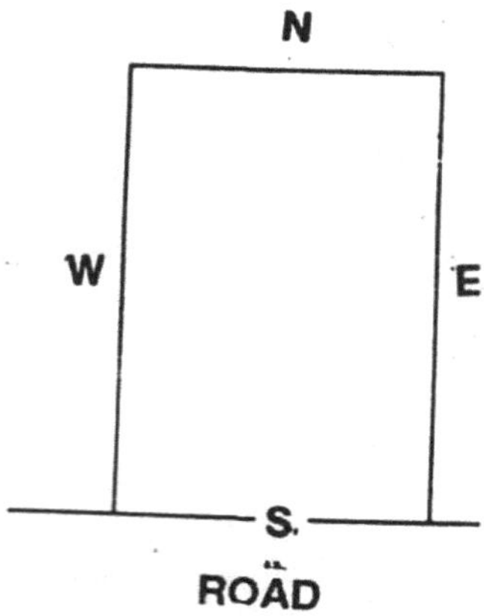

This is a rectangular plot & is of the best quality.

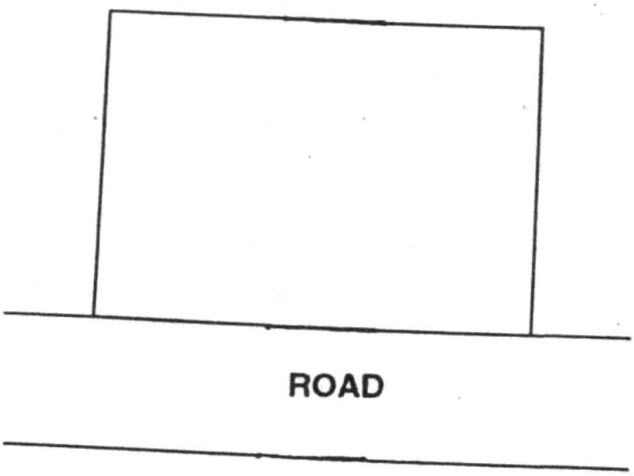

The wide open face plot is a good plot.

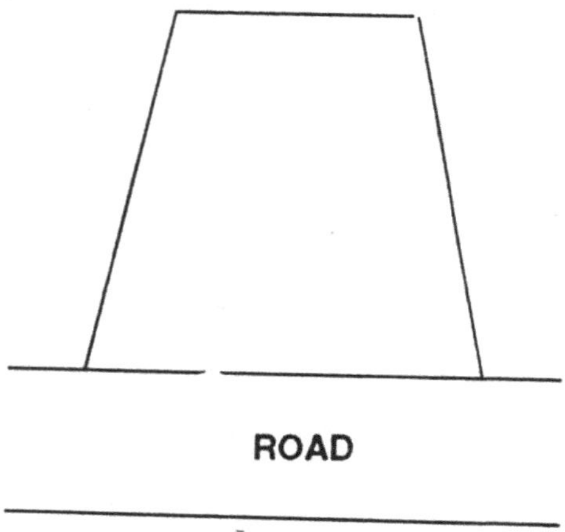

Gomukhi plot

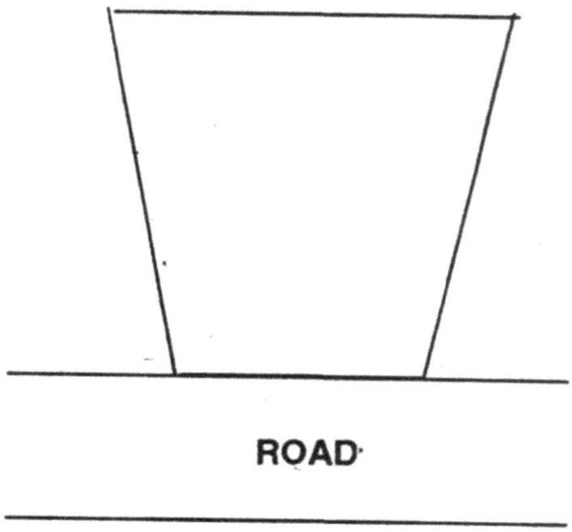

Shermukhi plot

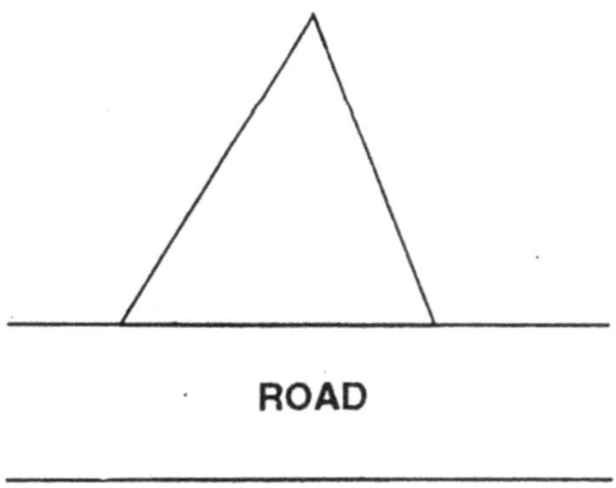

This is a triangular plot where not a single angle is of 90°. It is not a good plot.

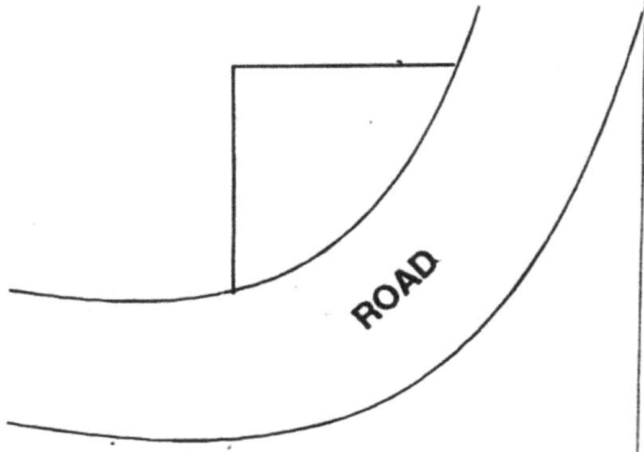

Semicircular plot. This plot is not good & is also with Vaastu fault.

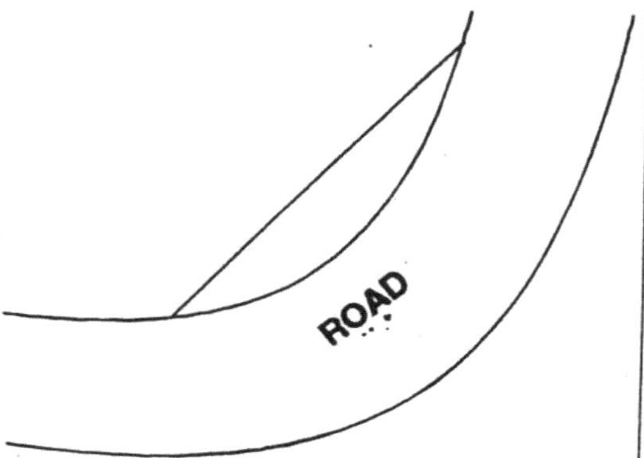

Bow-shaped plot indicates Vaastu fault.

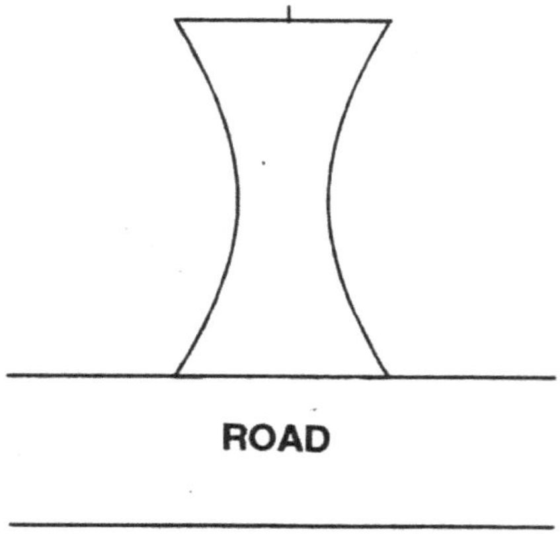

The plot which is very narrow in the middle. This type of plot is seen under the stairs which is used now a days as S.T.D. centre, tea shop or pan shop due to land scarcity.

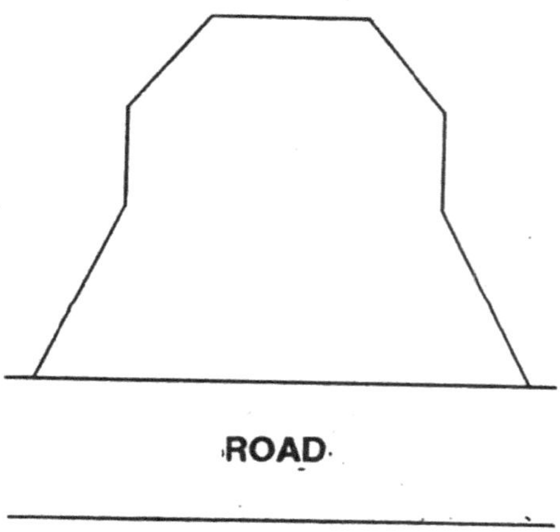

Multi angled plots. Such plots are in plenty around Howrah station of W. Bengal where there are many multi-cornered shops.

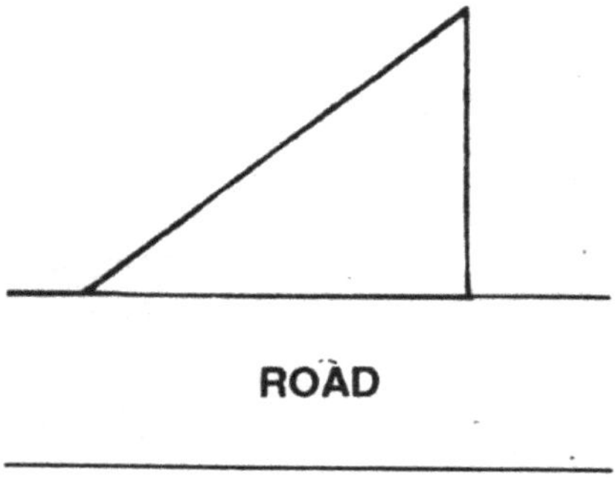

Triangular plot whose one angle is of 90° & other angle is of 45°.

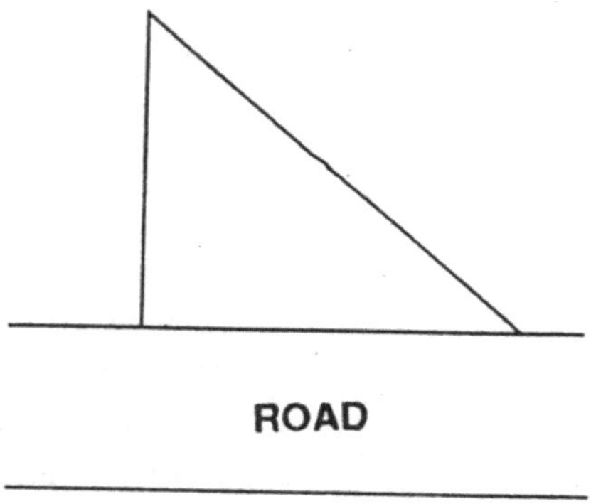

Triangular plot whose one angle is of 45° & other is of 90°.

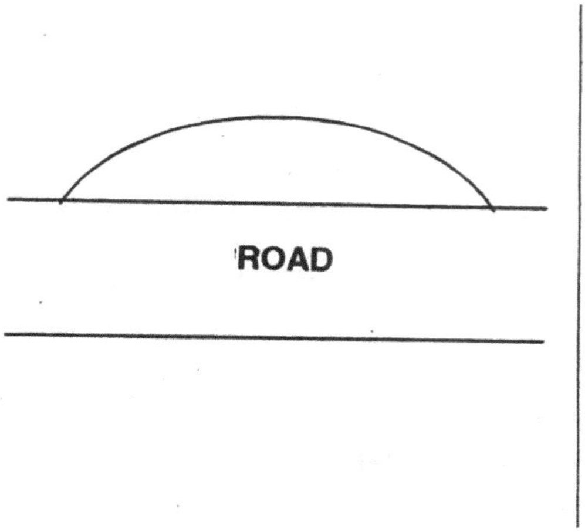

Moon shaped plot.

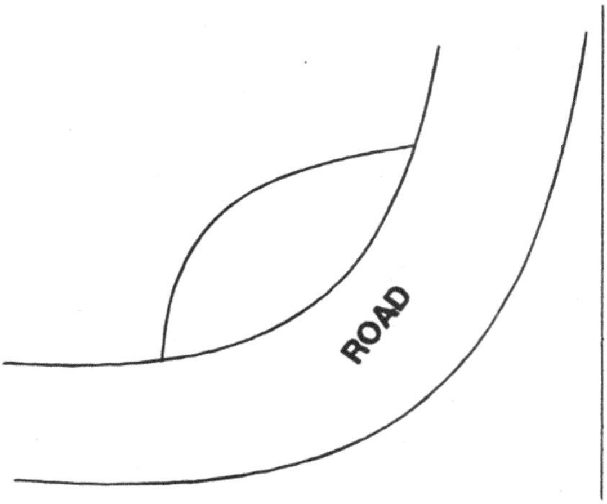

Moon shaped plot

Some Exceptions.

The man who works very hard is helped by malefic Rahu. Thus if in the Horoscope of a man Rahu enjoys exalted position then the faults of the direction can be removed. From a good Pandit you should take a lucky and auspicious time and lagan then start a business. During the lagan you should be happy and of free mind & you should call all your friends and relatives. The Landlord should wear new orange colour clothes. The auspicious time should be between 10-12 a.m. which is a time of young period of rising sun; and never in the night.

You should invite big people in the lagan or opening of business, the inner good waves of these big people will fall on your work & will be profitable.

You should become pious from mind, body and tongue and remembering your dynasty or family-God you should worship first God-Ganesh and make their permanent place in the right hand side of the shop. If you want to place the Gods above the counter or office or sitting place you can place it. You should remember that every thing should be new & from a good shop for the lagan of the shop. Same way the stationery should be new and Ledger Book should be started after putting swastik on the first page.

During the lagan time the complex should be decorated with flowers and rose water should be used maximum. The lamps should be lighted by ghee and scented Agarbatti should be used. The businessmen should know that their shop is another face of Goddess Lakshmi. So everything should be purified and sanctified.

The Shriyantra of eight elements is a symbol of Tripur sundri. It is said to be Lakshmi. As in the Nagara-Shrinagar, Shri in the God and human has increased the fame just like that shriyantra is the best yantra.

Kuber is God of wealth which is in the North face, so the money should be in the North side, you should keep one Rupee coin, some Gold & Silver always in the safe of your shop.

Industry Layout

Industry is of two types—one stands inside the town and other in the industrial area.

Town Industry—These industries are spread in the towns. These are on rent or on own land. The industry like plastic factory, sweet packets, and iron steel are there.

Industry in Industrial Area—The industries are rising in town very fast. Seeing this the Government has made a facility of separate industrial area outside the town. The government gives plot at reasonable prices for light & heavy industries. These plots hold important place in the Vaastu. The land and Vaastu law is applicable equally everywhere. Thus the plot chosen in the industrial area should be according to the Vaastu law, whether the industry is of light or heavy type. The position of machines is very important in the industry.

Main Machines' position

In the South West side. Which gives long life to the machines.

For illustration see next page

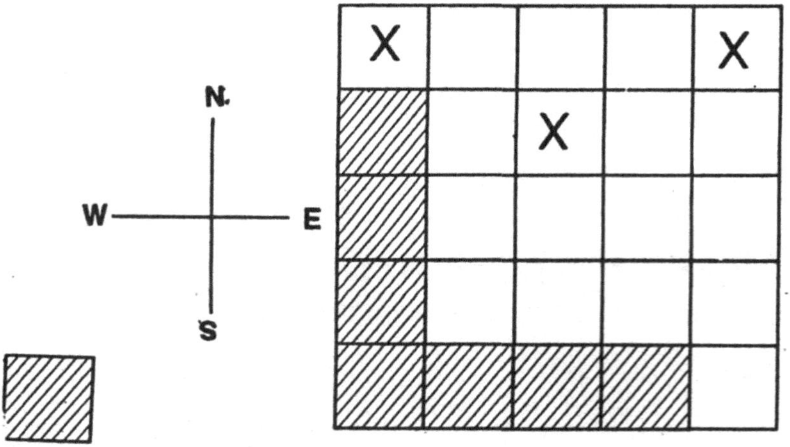

Place for Electricity, Boiler & Furniture

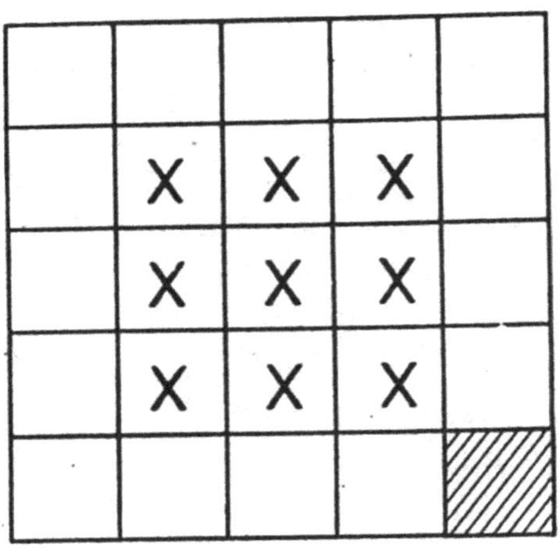

Place for source of electricity, boiler and furnace source. This angle gives heat, which is the Agnaya angle. There is a less chance of any accident.

Reception & Worship place

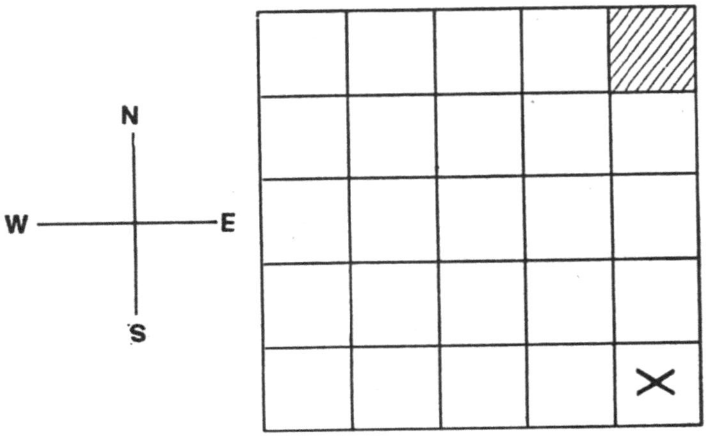

The Worship & reception should be in the Ishan side. This is a place of Gods & should be always purified. Never in the Agnaya angle.

Store room for Raw Materials

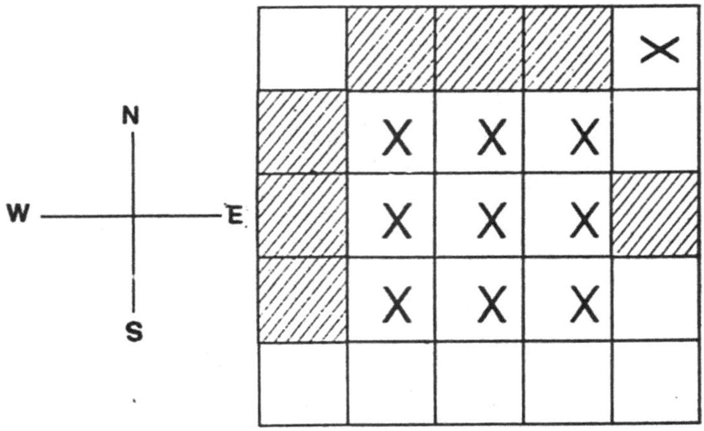

Middle North, middle West and some part of East are suitable for keeping raw materials for the factories. Not suitable for store room.

Place for finished goods

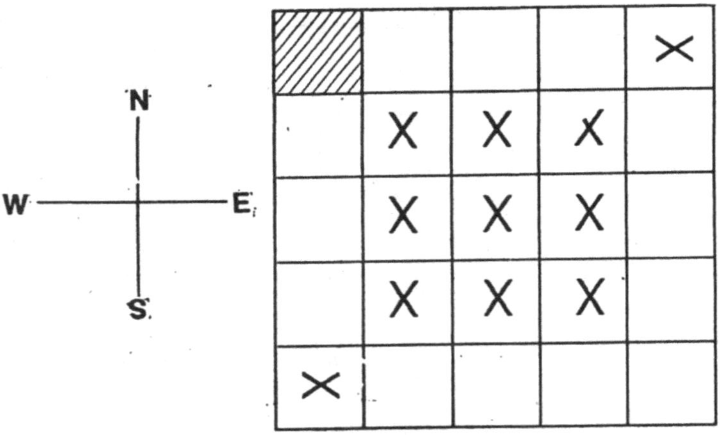

The finished goods always kept in the Wayava part will be sold quickly & the glaze of the goods would be maintained.

Ishan, Nairithya & middle part of the plot is not suitable for finished goods. The goods won't be sold quickly.

Main office

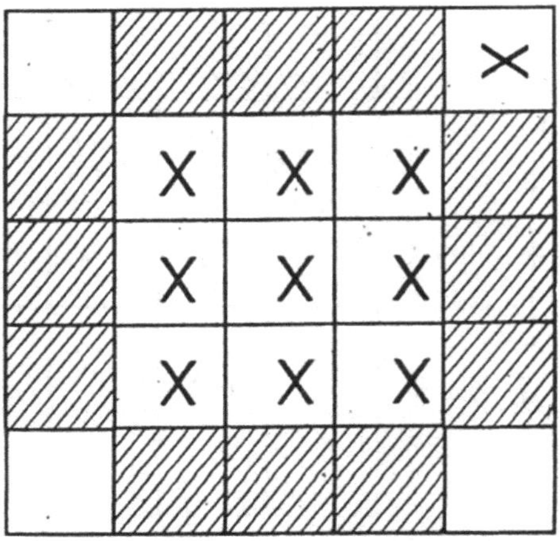

The middle parts of North, East, South & West are suitable for the main office of the factory.

The East and West part of the plot is best for the main office.

North-East or Ishan and the middle of the plot is not suitable for the main office. Wrong decisions would be taken here. The workers would be always hostile with the committee and there would always be a strike in the factory.

House for gate keepers & workers

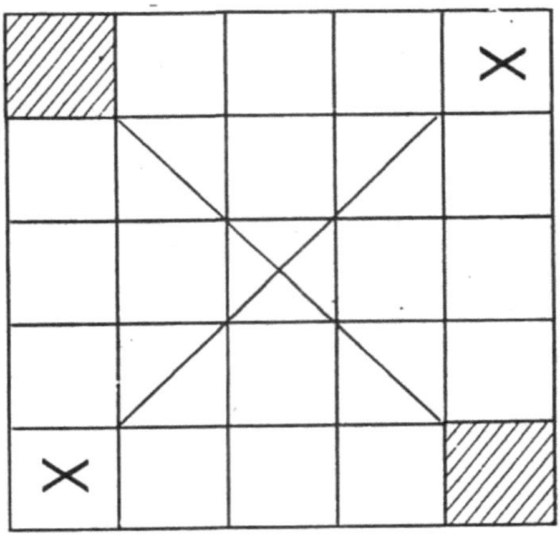

Agnaya part is for the night watchmen & gatekeepers. Here the night watchmen would not get any sleep and will watch the factory nicely. Wayava is for the workers; they will work hard the whole day & will get a nice & peaceful sleep in the night here. North-East, South-West, and middle of the plot are not suitable for the workers and gatekeepers.

Some Rules

(1) The door keepers or the guard room should be near the door of the factory, keeping in mind the direction of the main gate. If the main gate is in the North then the room should be in the West, if in the East then in the South, if in the West then in the North, if in the South then in the East.

(2) The administration office should be in the specific place and main head should sit in the South West or South East. Technical office & the accountants office should be in the East, North or South-East, Sales Officer, the guard or the temporary workers should sit North-West of the main office.

(3) North-East should be kept apart for the waiting room or

Reception room for the guests. Or keep it vacant for the little bit of greenary.

(4) For the measurements of the goods North West is the best suited site but on the temporary basis North East can be used.

(5) For water processing North-East is the best place.

(6) For transport North-West or South-East is suitable place.

Thus we can say that for running any industry successfully, some Vaastu laws should be observed.

Hotels & Restaurants

Hotels & restaurants are related to the food & are made in the complexes. This business is very sensitive as this business should be done on the plot full of Vaastu law otherwise the food won't be tasty and the customers will be restless even while sitting.

Main rules—

(1) In a residential Hotel for every room it is not necessary to have bathrooms in the North-East but entrance doors or balconies can be made there.

(2) North East should be kept empty, as far as possible, or can be used for the reception hall for guests.

(3) Dining room in the West part and kitchen in the Agnaya angle. If not possiable in the Agnaya angle, then it can be made in North West near the dining room.

(4) In the whole building it is not suitable to build rooms in the North-East part.

(5) The entrance can be made in the North or East so that door Mandap can be made.

Place for entrance door.

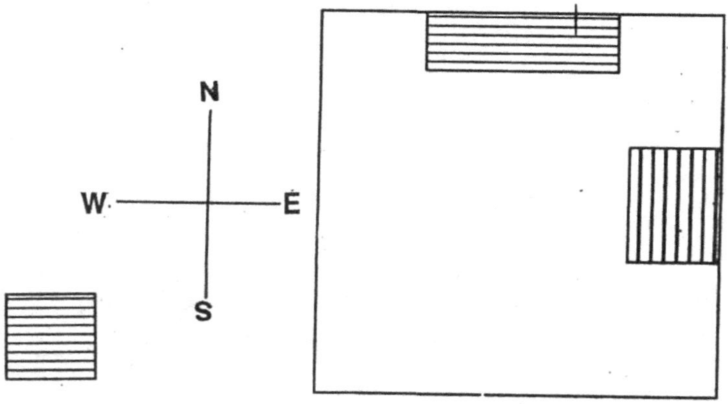

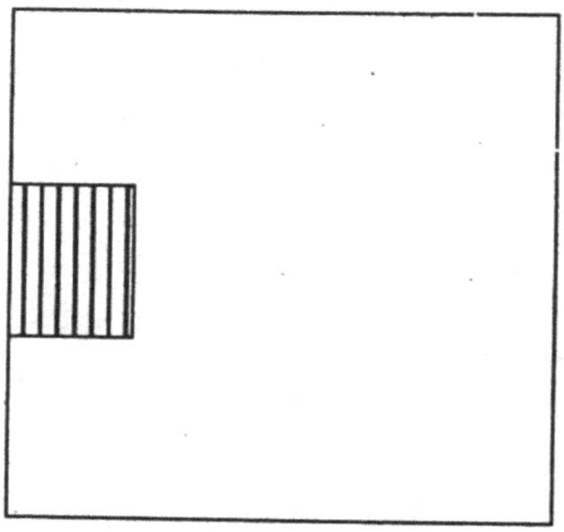

Arrangements for food.

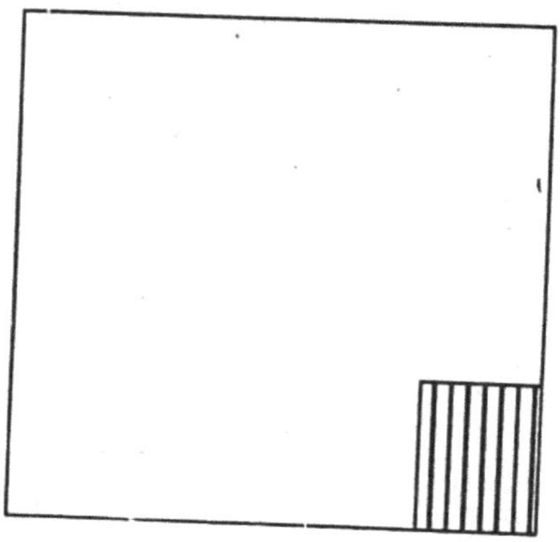

Arrangements for kitchen.

(6) If it is a hotel with stars then a swimming pool is neccessary so it should be in the North-East, West or North or East. Swimming pool increases the beauty of hotels.

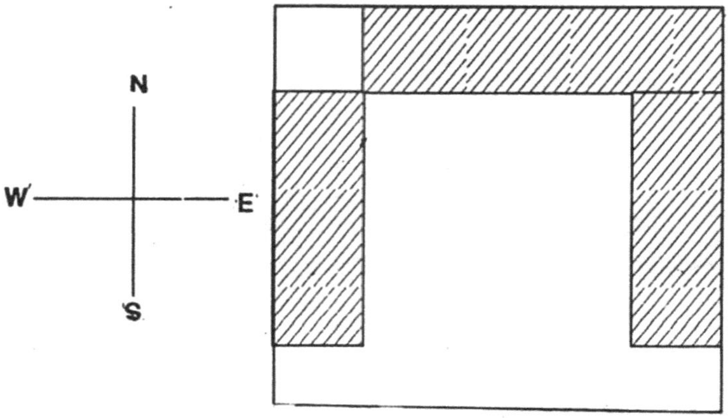

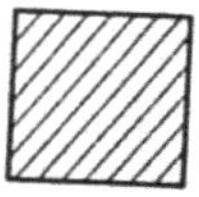

Suitable for swimming pool, the water will be good nice and healthy here. No fear of accidents.

(7) One hall-room which is neccessary for the reception or parties or conferences; should be in the North West.

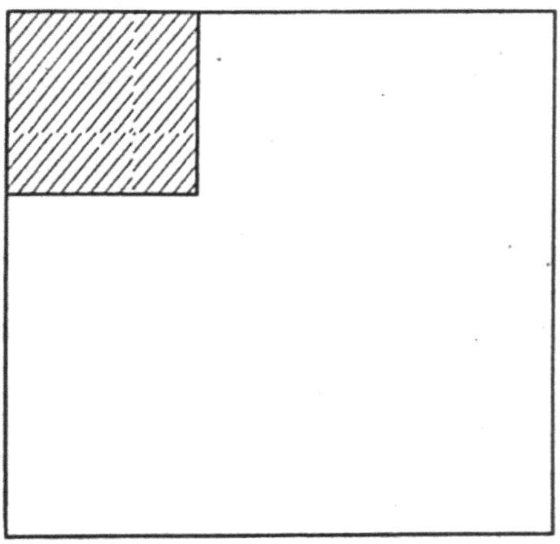

Best suited for the hall.

Results of High & Low Plots

The high & low plots according to directions provide results in differents ways, which we can know by following ways :—

(1) If Ishan is high— If the Ishan which is a place for worship is high then the landlord gets bankrupt.

(2) If Wayava is high— If this place is higher than the Agnaya, then it is unlucky & if higher than the Ishan then we get success from all the sides.

(3) If Agnaya is high— If higher than Nairithya then bad and if higher than Ishan & Wayava then wealth comes from everywhere.

(4) If Nairithya is high— If the nairithya is high then we get fame, prosperity and wealth.

(5) If North is high— Then the landlord's prosperity is lost.

(6) If South is high— Then the people residing there get fame & prosperity and their health is always good.

(7) If East is high— Then the generation is heading towards the end & only girl child is born.

(8) If West is high— Then there is an increase in fame & generation.

(9) If Ishan is low— Then, from everywhere, there is flow of happiness, fame & prosperity.

(10) If Wayava is low— If lower than Nairithya & Agnaya then it is very lucky but if lower than Ishan then it gives birth to enmity

& diseases.

(11) If Agnaya is low—If lower than the Wayava & Ishan then there is a chance of accident, bad health and enmity; but if lower than the Nairithya then gives good results.

(12). If Nairithya is low—Then there is a chance of sudden death, diseases and body disorders.

(13) If North is low—Then there is gain of wealth.

(14) If South is low—Then there is loss of health & wealth.

(15) If East is low—Then it will give fame, prosperity and long life. The landlord is happy.

(16) If West is low—Then it is very unlucky & gives death & diseases.

The results of closing the corners of Boundary wall

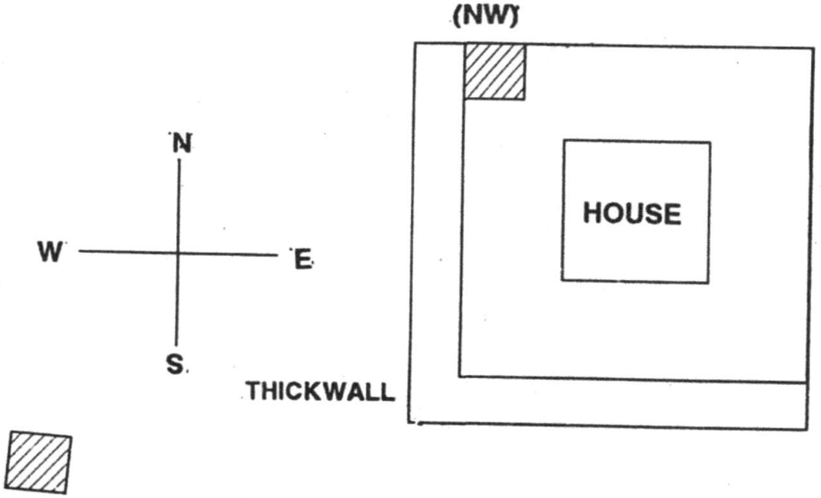

The Wayava angle should not be closed. If it is closed, then many accidents occur in ceramic industry or mechanical factories.

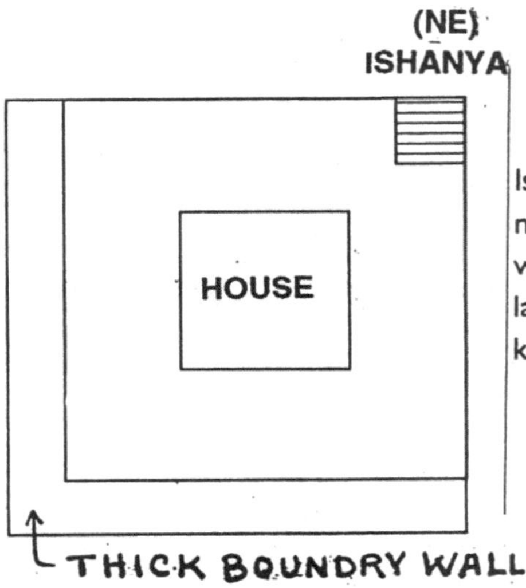

Ishan angle should never be closed or nor any heavy thing should be kept; which reflects very badly on the landlord. Thus this place should be kept empty.

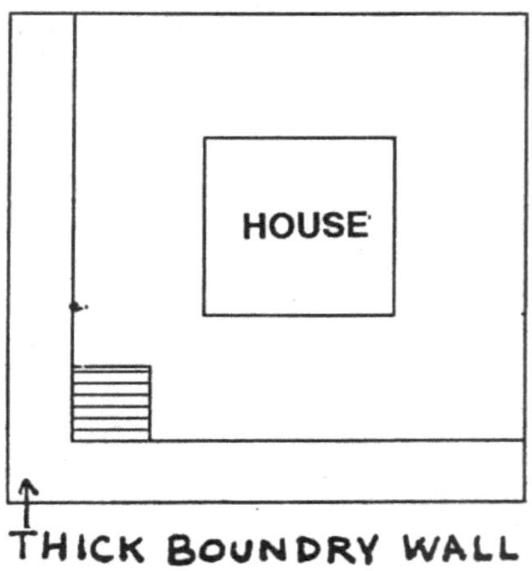

The construction can be done in the Nairithya or heavy things can be stored here.

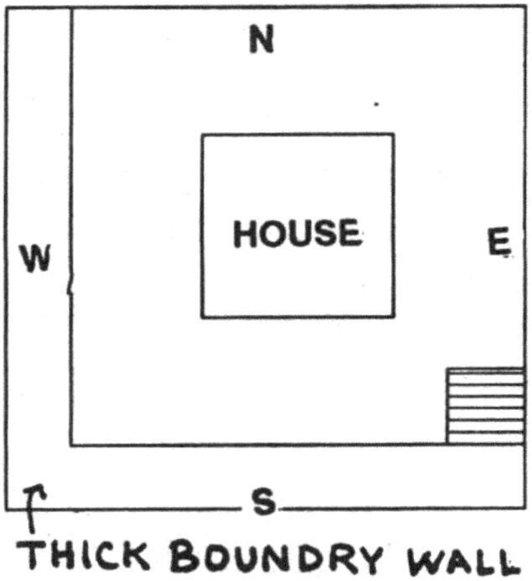

The Agnaya angle should never be closed by construction which can result in fire accidents & decrease in the business.

Thus we can conclude from the above discussion, that the angle made according to the Vaastu is good and will result in good.

Tin shed & Asbestos.

Some people according to their own facility puts tin or asbestos sheds on their houses. But these sheds are made by following the direction of wind. Otherwise there will be the chance of damage.

Some sheds are—

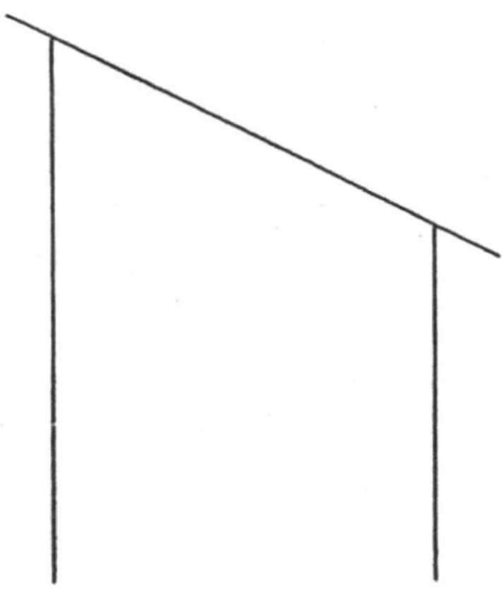

This slope should be towards the North or East so that shed should not be flown away by the wind from the Wayava or West.

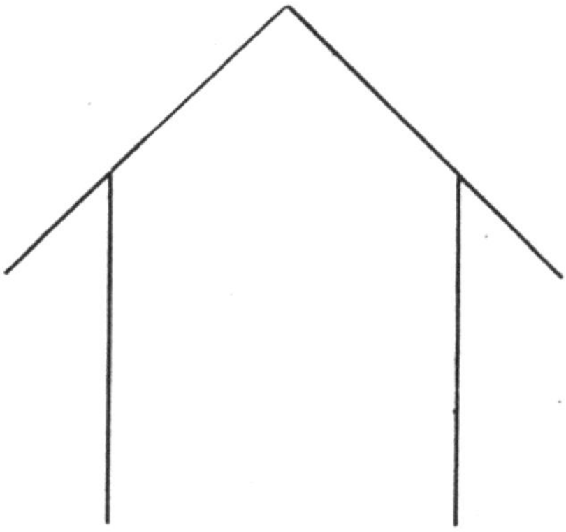

This slope should be uniform in the North South or East West. Such type of sheds are commonly seen in the villages.

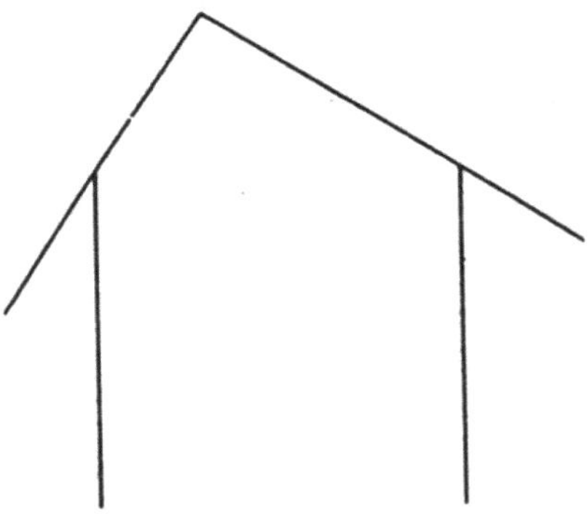

More slope in the North & East and less slope in the South & West. Such type of sheds are used to increase the height of the house and usually used in the schools of villages.

Besides these, many types of slopy sheds are made. Where there is more rain or snow, these types of sheds are seen as in-Assam, Manipur, Meghalay, Darjeeling, Kashmir & other hilly areas. These types of sheds are used in the earthquake prone areas.

Twin House

In the Hindu customs & rituals twin fruits are unlucky. Same way twin house is very unlucky.

Sometimes two friends to save money make twin house on the same plot with one partition wall. I have seen these houses in the M.P. Housing Colony of Janta & L.I.G. flats. This way with one wall the one house is full of faults and the other is good even while the interior plans and facilities are identical. In this one landlord is very good and the other goes down declining.

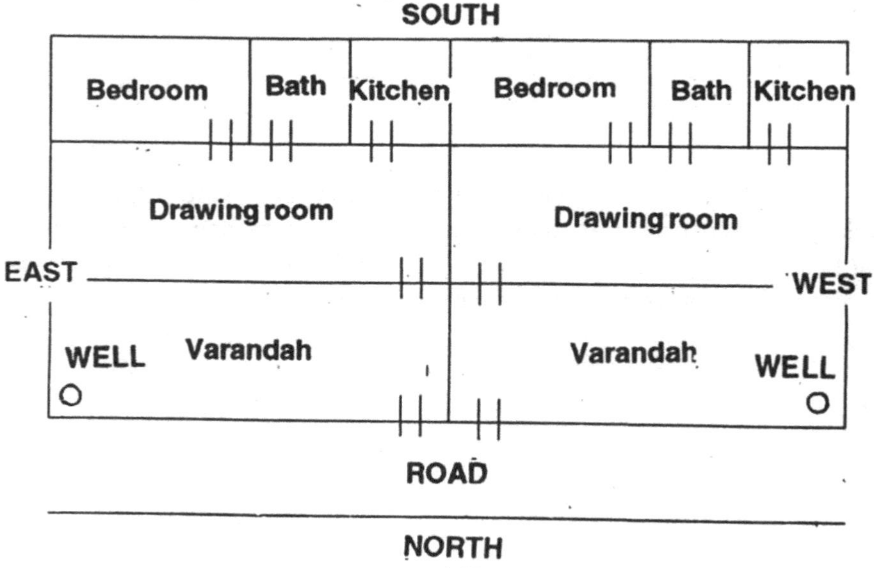

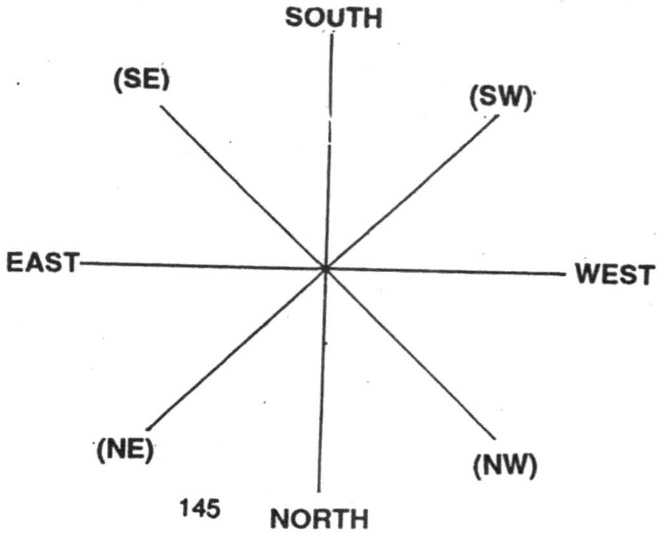

(1) The above both houses have same plan inside.
(2) Both houses have one wall which is used by both the families alike.
(3) In this twin-house, one house is according to the Vaastu and the other is faulty. So, as far as possible, twin house should not

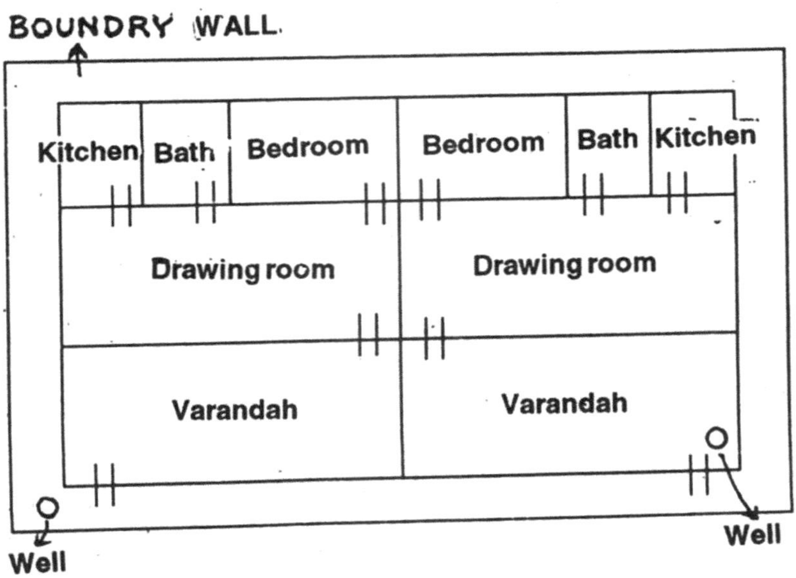

be built in any case as one might have Vaastu fault.

(4) Sometimes both the houses become faulty because Vaastu-rules have not been applied to them.

(5) If you make twin houses, or colonies or multistory building each flat should be according to the Vaastu.

(6) "A" house has both houses with Vaastu faults. There no Vaastu-law was applied while doing construction, even though two houses have same planning inside.

(7) 'B' twin house is made according to the Vaastu-law the 'C' is a Vaastu house and D is with fault. In this plot one house is good & the other is with fault.

East-Faced House

East-faced house is said to be the king of the houses. Its importance is as follows.

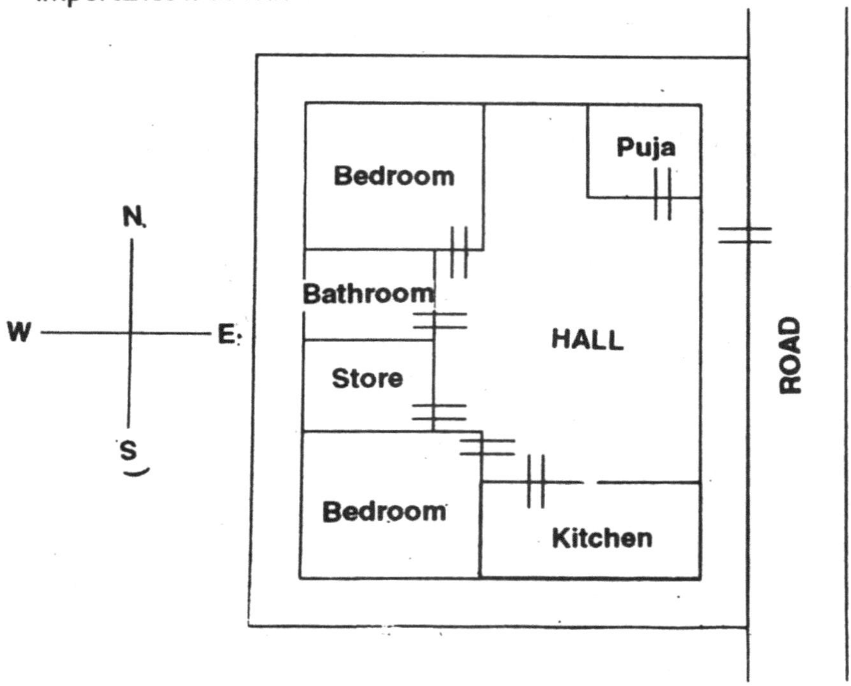

(1) East faced house is of the best quality. While going, out of the house in morning you can see the Sun automatically which is very good. This house helps in increase of wealth & generation. Sons born at this place are very good & helpful to their fathers. In the East-faced Neelkantha bird is always seen.

(2) The land of East should be low in the East faced house.

(3) You should leave equal space all a round the house in the East faced house so that the children of the house should not have any problems.

(4) If any door of the house is in the Agnaya side of the East faced house then the landlord faces lots of problems. There will be fear of fire & theft. There will always be loss of money.

(5) If the outer platform is higher than the floor of the house then the landlord faces the problem of cough & debt.

(6) There should be no dirty things and garbage in the East part.

(7) While making the East faced house they should observe full Vaastu laws and maintain certain laws which should be told to the architect.

(a)	Ishan	Puja room
(b)	Wayava	Bed room
(c)	West	Bath room
(d)	West	Store room
(e)	Nairithya	Bed room
(f)	Agnaya	Kitchen
(g)	East	Hall

According to the above laws the architect will provide you with a perfect plan. And if you make a house according to this plan, you will live a happy life.

West-Faced House

West faced house is superior to the king like East faced house. Its facilities & importance is as following.

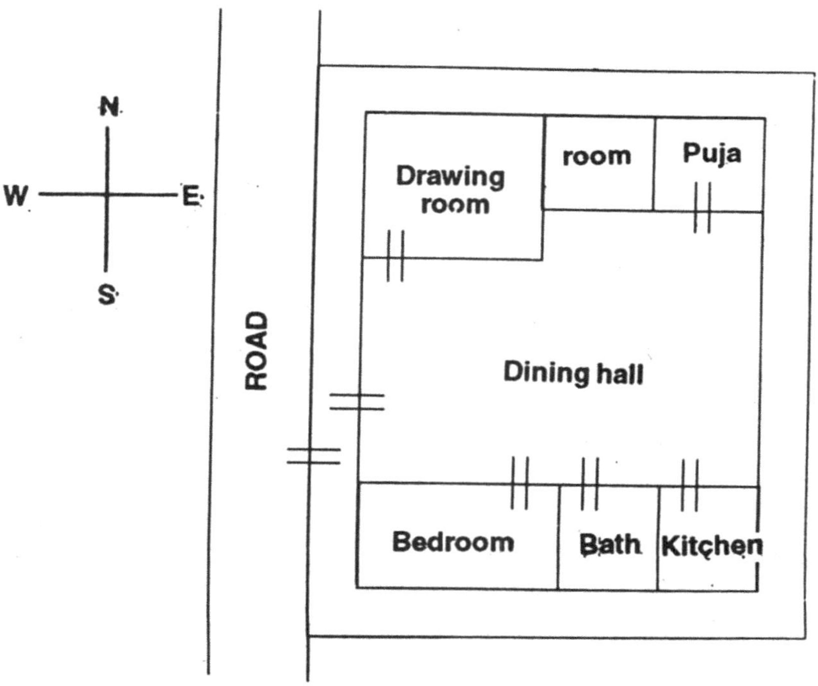

(1) It is said to be a good quality house.

(2) This West faced house gives all the prosperity, fame and wealth to the landlord.

(3)	Ishan	Worship place
(4)	Wayava	Sitting room
(5)	West	Main door
(6)	Nairithya	Sleeping room
(7)	South	Bathroom
(8)	Agnaya	Kitchen
(9)	North	Rooms
(10)	Middle portion should be kept empty, and can be used as sitting room or dining room, when needed.	

West faced house is full of happiness.

North-Faced House

The North faced house gives plenty of prosperity & fame. But the house should be according to the Vaastu principles.

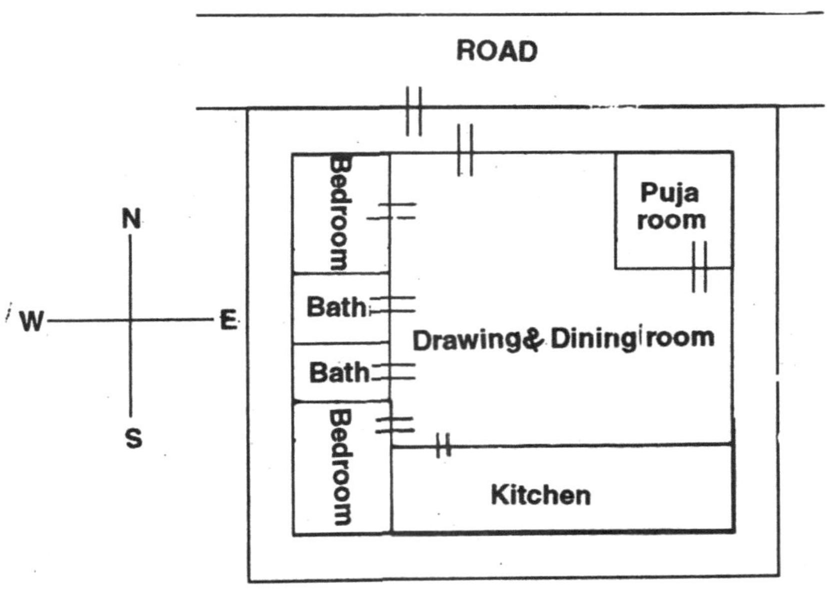

(1)	Ishan	Puja room
(2)	East	Sitting room
(3)	Agnaya	Kitchen
(4)	South	Sleeping room
(5)	Nairithya	Sleeping room
(6)	West	Bath room
(7)	Wayava	Sleeping room
(8)	North	Main door.

The females of house get immense happiness. The wealth continues accumulating. The landlord gets the pleasure of going to the pilgrimage. To get all the facility and results of the North faced house, the house should be made according to the Vaastu law. While applying the Vaastu law, the direction faults are eliminated.

South-Faced House

The South-faced house is not said to be good but if the house is built according to the Vaastu it can be modified and altered.

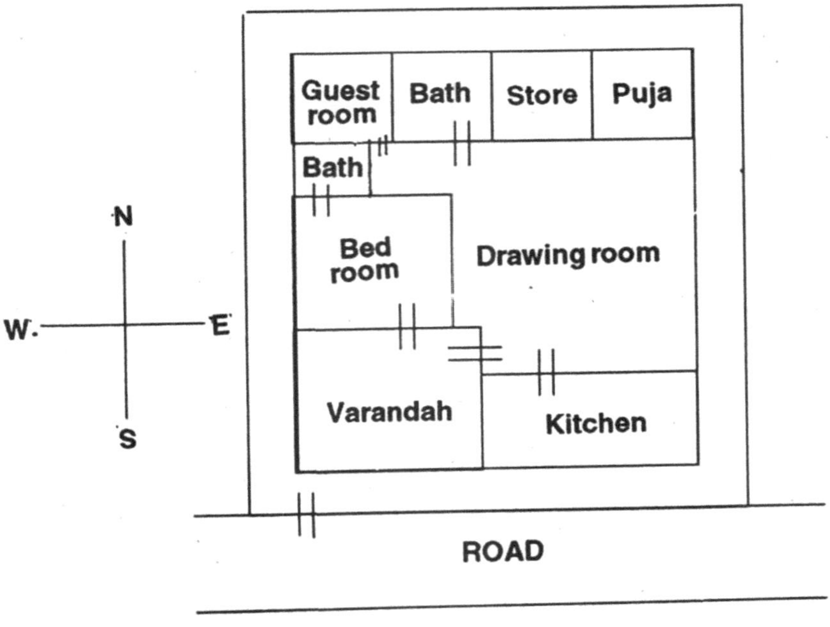

The above house is safe from the Vaastu fault; because the South is said to be the door of death even then, this house is good and gives the landlord wealth & prosperity.

(1)	East	Sitting room
(2)	Ishan	Puja room
(3)	North	Store room
(4)	Agnaya	Kitchen
(5)	West	Bath room
(6)	West	Sleeping room
(7)	Nairithya	Verandah
(8)	Wayava	Guest room.

Here South-faced house has been wisely designed, by using Vaastu-oriented techniques. Hence the said house can be rightly termed as an ideal house.

Ishan-Faced House

While making the Ishan-faced house one has to be extra cautious because this direction is said to be very auspicious. Puja place should always be in this place.

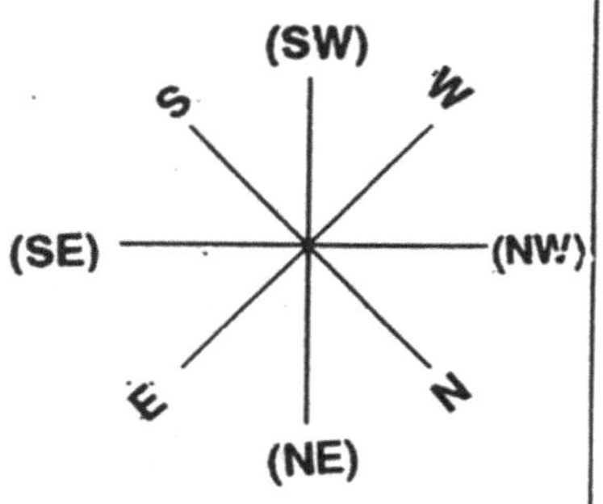

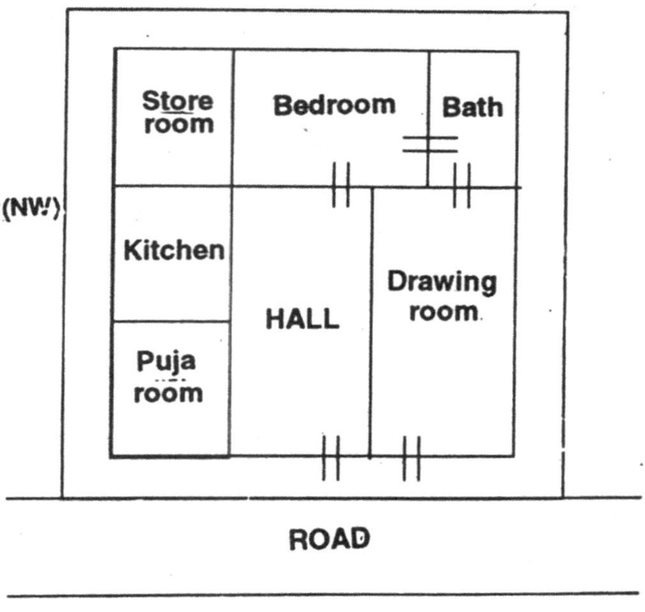

(1) The puja place should be to the left of the entrance door.

(2)	East Ishan	Entrance door
(3)	North Ishan	Drawing room
(4)	West	Bath room
(5)	Nairathya	Bed room
(6)	South	Store room
(7)	Agnaya	Kitchen

(8) The middle place is kept empty for the hall.

Ishan is an angle which is situated in midway of North and East. It is difficult to construct a house by making epicentre of angle-faced plot according to principles of Vaastu. But such plots are generally found now. A lot of caution is required to utilise angles of other directions. Residents, living on a plot of Ishan-angle are spiritual persons who have abiding faith in God. This plot can be the noblest piece of land, if purity is maintained. I have seen renowned personalities of world prospering under an Ishan-faced house.

Wayava-Faced House

In wayava-faced house there is an abundance of air thus this angle is a healthy angle. In this angle there should be lesser rooms made with care, as far as possible within Vaastu laws.

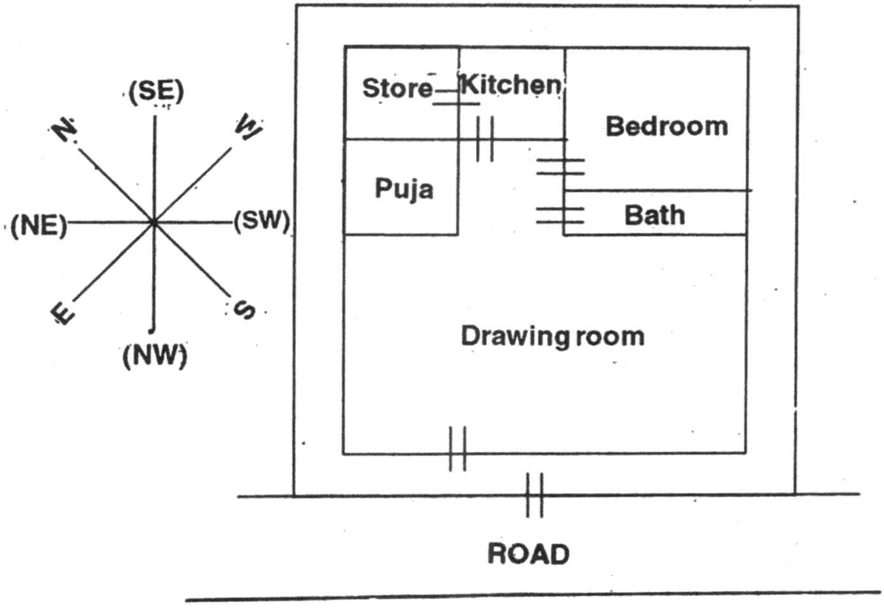

(1)	Wayava & Middle of West	Sitting room
(2)	Nairithya	Bath room
(3)	South & Nairithya	Sleeping room
(4)	Agnaya	Kitchen
(5)	East	Store room
(6)	Ishan	Puja room
(7)	Middle part of plot & North	Sitting room.

This direction is very powerful. In this place you can become a very rich man or you can even be a pauper, starving even for a morsel. So while making a Wayava faced house you have to observe the Vaastu-laws.

Agnaya Faced House

The lord of this angle is Ganesh. This direction is very fruitful for children and wife but agnaya angle is very dangerous also. This angle is an angle of accidents and deaths, if house is not made according to the Vaastu laws.

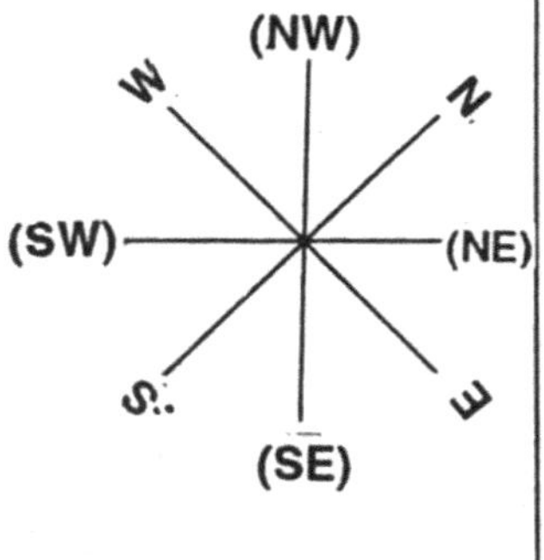

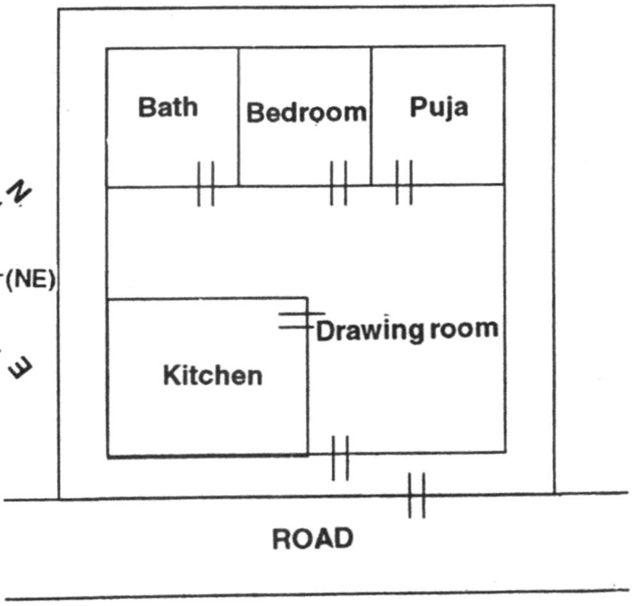

(1)	South	Kitchen
(2)	Agnaya	Sitting room
(3)	Ishan	Puja room
(4)	Wayava	Sleeping room
(5)	West	Bath room
(6)	Nairithya	Kept empty

It has been noticed that people often do construct house on Aganaya-faced plot. The residents of such houses are found to be restive.

The aforesaid house- plan was drafted as per the vaastu-laws, despite this it is advisable to avoid, as far as possible to abandon such a plot.

Nairithya Faced House

The lord of Nairithya is khetrapal. This direction is taken to be the best. If the house is made, according to the Vaastu, then it is full of joy or delights. The husband gets the pleasure of wife and children are peaceful & prosperous.

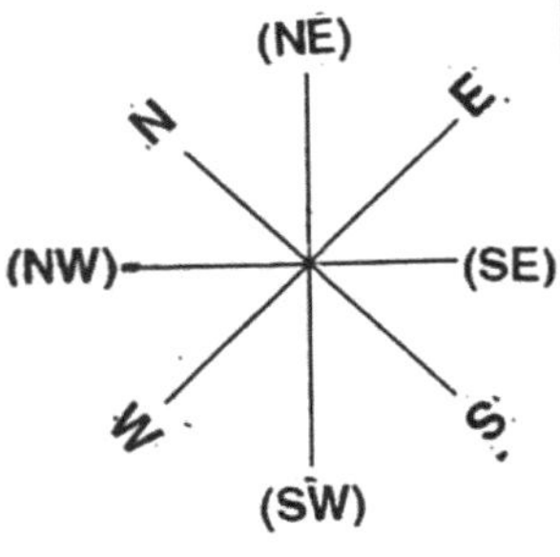

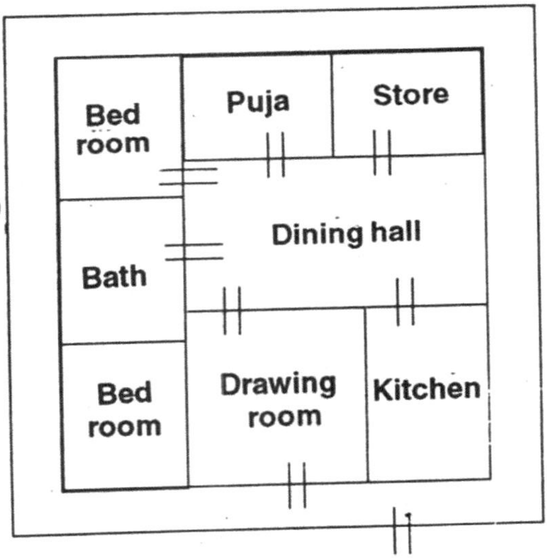

(1)	South Agnaya	Kitchen
(2)	East Agnaya	Dining room
(3)	Ishan	Puja room
(4)	North	Sleeping room
(5)	Wayava	Bath room
(6)	West	Sleeping room
(7)	Nairithya	Sitting room

The above house is full of Vaastu laws and this construction will give prosperity to the landlord.

Plot on two pathways

In the beginning we have studied about the plot on one pathway. Now we will study about the plot on two pathways or roads

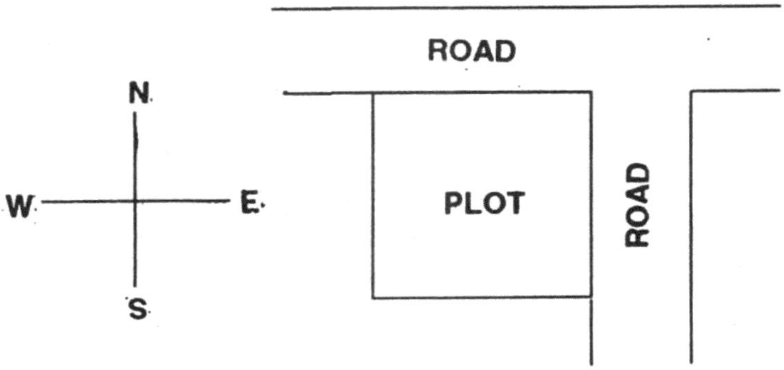

This plot has one path from East & the other goes to West. In this way a plot has pathways North faced & East-faced and is very lucky & of best quality.

This plot has one way in the West & other in South, so this plot is both South-faced & West faced plot. This is an ordinary type of plot.

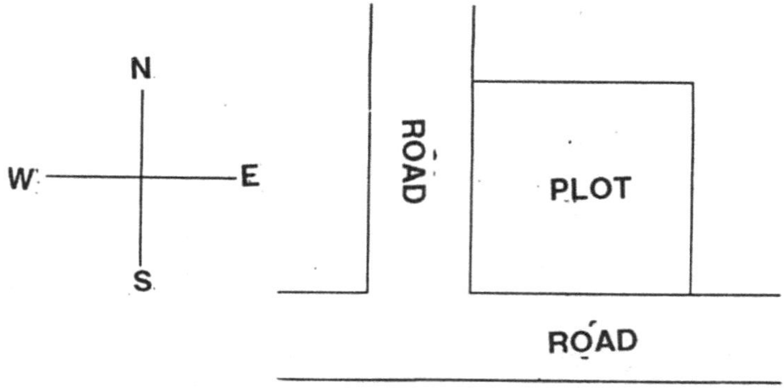

This plot has one way in the North & other in the West. So this plot is west & north faced plot. This type of plot gives ordinary results.

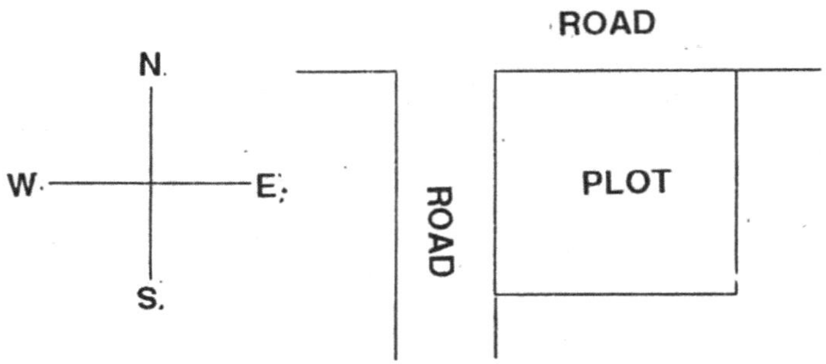

This plot is South faced & East faced plot because its one way is in South & the other in the East. This plot is good due to East-faced direction.

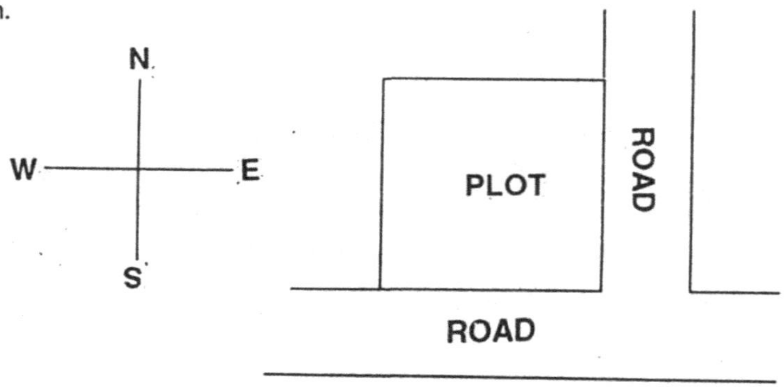

The above four plots are with two pathways joined together with one another and now we will study about the plots having two roads on opposite parts.

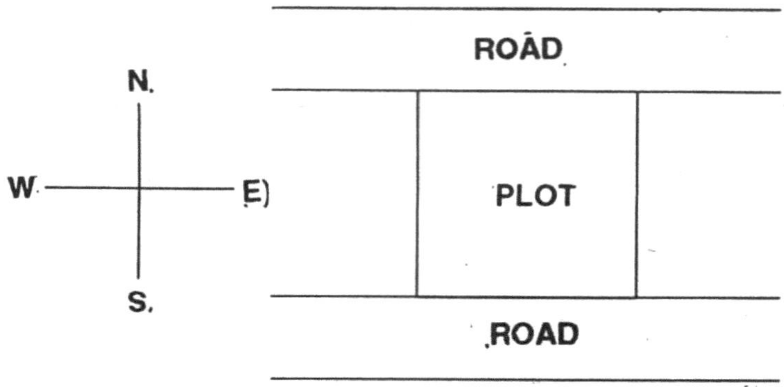

This plot has one road in the North & one in the South, & the plot is North-faced & South-faced plot which is not good according to the Vaastu law.

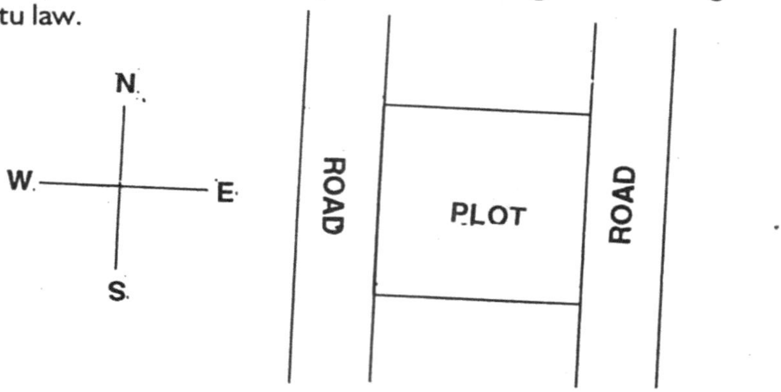

This plot is West-faced & East-faced plot because one road is in the East & other in the West. This plot gives normal results.

THREE PATHWAYS PLOT

This has been formed by three roads emanating from East, West & North. So this plot is East-faced North faced & West-faced plot which is said not to be a good plot.

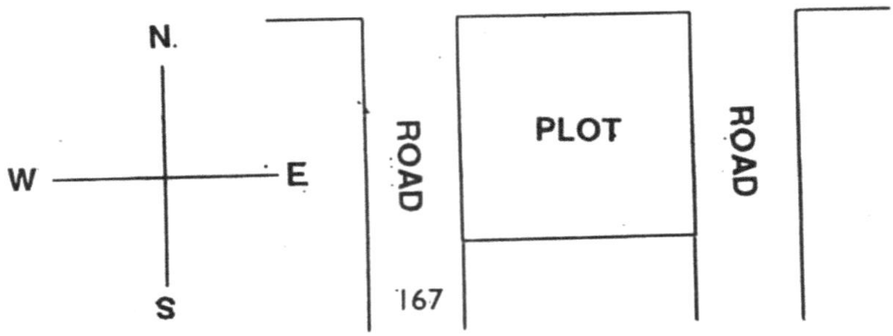

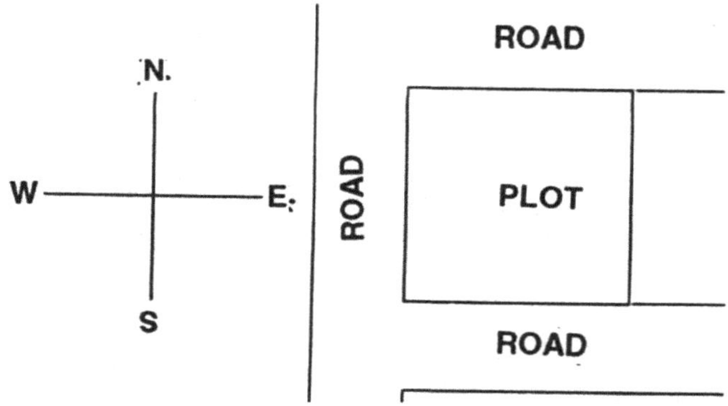

Three roads, from North, West and South form a plot which is called a North-faced, South-faced and West-faced plot which is not a good plot hence it is better to remain without such a plot.

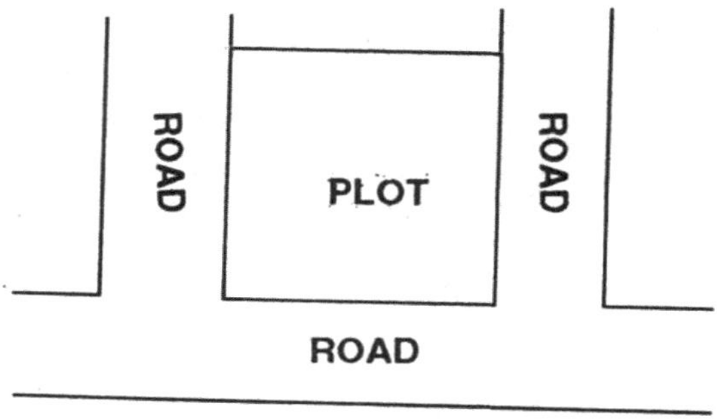

This plot is formed by roads coming from West South and East which is not a good plot. The landlord will always be disturbed by noise.

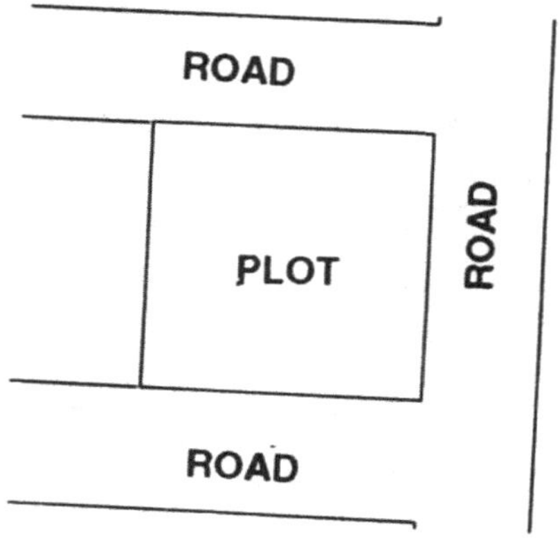

This is a plot formed by the roads coming from North, East & South, so this plot is called East faced, North faced & South faced which is good plot of medium category.

Plot in junction of four roads

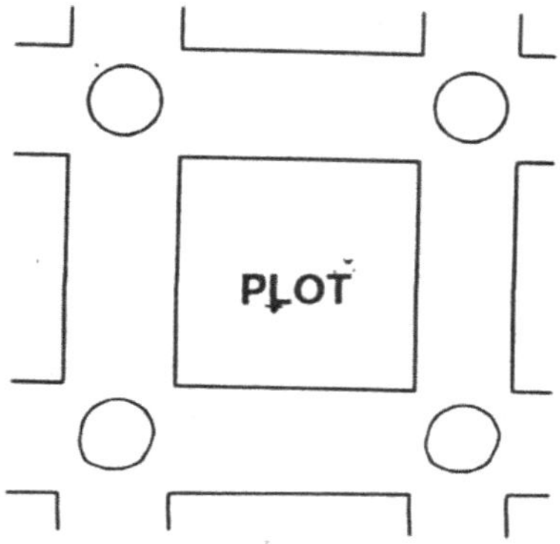

This is a peculiar plot whose all the four angles are having joint place which is not good. But from the view-point of business this plot will prove a miracle. This plot is a boon for a multistory building. But a normal person will suffer many problems if he builds a house here.

Plot in middle of Four Joints

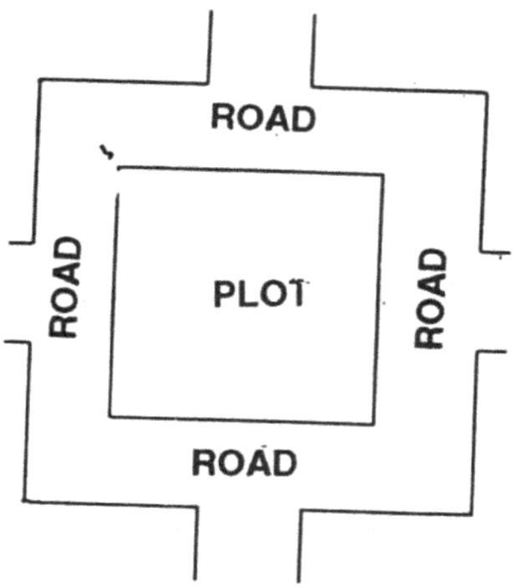

This plot has path Vedh fault in the four joints which is not good.

Auspicious Day & Puja

Before starting Vaastu work, some auspicious day should be nominated by some pandits or brahamins whether the planets of the landlord are good or not as such a work is not the job of a Vaastu shastri. Though this is done by pandits or astrologers yet I am giving some general & brief account of auspicious time.

This is enough for the landlord to know how auspicious day is worked out or what are its purposes and procedures.

Normally, for the time of foundation laying, construction work acquisition starting & fixation of main door & Griha Pravesh you should consult an astrologer for every thing and an auspicious day and time for everything is worked out.

The old house which has outlived its utility 1sttime also starts giving unlucky fruits and if so, then at that time Vaastu shanti should be done.It is said that life of house depends on the standard of material used. While constructing a house if high quality of raw materials is used then the house has a long life.

Now firstly according to the "khatarambh" muhurat foundation should be laid. You should first put, in a plate of copper, soil, gold, five gems, saptdhanya etc and on top of that put the stone or brick from foundation site. At the time of khanan (Digging) you should always see the position of Rahumukh, after that only you should think about the sun rays in the rahu-chakra.

Opinion of Teachers (GURUS)

Actually our ancestor gurus had discovered this secret shastra for our better & happy life. With the time this shastra reached its zenith. The man's life was disciplined and there was happiness all around. It is a principle that if a man becomes regular he also becomes careless. Thus, we again became careless by which this shastra drifted away from us. It is then that there is fall & alternate rise. This will go on till eternity.

(1) If sun is in Singh, Kanya or Tula rasi, then you should dig in Agnaya.
(2) If sun is in Vreshickik, Dhanu or Makar rasi then dig in the Ishan.
(3) If sun is in the Kumbh, Mean or Mesh rasi then dig in the Wayava.
(4) If sun is in the Vrish, Mithun & Kark rasi then dig in the Nairithya.

If foundation is laid in the Devsayan period & prithvisayan period it was said to be bad. Devsayan is in the middle of Ashwin month of shukl Ekadashi to Kartik shukl Ekadashi; And prithvisayan is on 5th, 7th 9th, 10th, 12th, 21st , 24th , 26th days from the planet of sun of the month.

Best Muhurat for foundation time

It is necessary to know when foundation should be laid. Thursday falling the shukla pakhsha of Vaishakh, Shravan, Paush, Phalgun, and Margshirsha Nakhshatras or when Thursday falls in Pushya, Shravan, Rohini, Mrigshera,Ashlesha, Purvasharha Nakhshatras,then this is a best muhurat for foundation.

(1) Confluence of rohini, chitra, anuradha, hasta, uttar phalguni planets & Wednesday.
(2) Day should be Wednesday, Thursday or Friday.
(3) Leaving evening time, during day when the sun is in the sky.
(4) Shuklapakhsha.
(5) When sun is in uttarayan.

According to the command of Gurus you should worship with your wife the lords–Ganapati, Vishnu, Mahesh, Dikpal Shodash Kalash of sixteen female deities, kshtrapati and Kuldevta.

After the house construction the main festival is griha pravesh and for this you should find out good & lucky Muhurat from pandits.

For Griha Pravesh Auspicious Dates & Months

The grihapravesh should be at the auspicious day & time after doing pooja & purifying rituals.

While going inside the house (the grihapravesh) you should do the puja of 81 pad of Vaastu from a team of great & best intelligent Brahamins and then put kalash, full of water & coconut on top & after seeing a face of lucky or auspicious lady enter the house.

The main door should be decorated with flowers and kalash with leaves. With the chanting of auspicious songs by the ladies one should enter the house with a desire to live in the house during that night and thereafter. Where there are no windows, doors and there is no roof made till now or there is no puja rituals done, then we should not enter this house.

One should wear neat & clean clothes & enter the house with Brahamins reciting vedas sanskrit rhymes.

After that you should satiate to the Brahmins, astrologers and the architects by giving them moral respect & honour.

Vaishakh, Shavan, Paush, Phalgun & margshirsh month are lucky months to enter a new house.

(1) Guruwar (Thursday) pushya, Shavan, rohini, mrigshira ashlasha, purbashada planets & Thursday all these should

combine together to give auspicious day & time.

(2) The day should be of rohini, chitra, anuradha, hast, Uttarphaiguni planets joined with Wednesday.

(3) The days should be Thursday, Wednesday & Friday.

(4) The time should be day time leaving evening time.

(5) Time should be in Shuklapakhsha.

(6) Surya should be in the North direction.

You should remember that at this time the husband & wife should wear neat & clean clothes & should wear gold jewelry. In happy & joy mood they should enter the house with thier friends, relatives, well wishers and some brahmins and with some auspicious or lucky ladies. You should take good wishes & blessings of brahamins, elders & the Gurus.

The main door should be ornamented by vandanvar & kalash Toran.

Some Laws for Residence

If the house, the plot & the soil is built according to the Vaastu shastra, then some Vaastu law has to be maintained by the people living in it.

(1) While sleeping your head should be in the South or East.

(2) There should not be harsh noise while closing or opening doors.

(3) There should be no jug or jar, full of water, near telephone stand because the telephone sound produces electrical rays which are hot & harmful to the water.

(4) The important papers should be always kept in an almirah kept in the East side, otherwise the related events will not be to your benefit.

(5) There is a neccessity of locker in a house in the Ishan side.

(6) The food, should be made facing East, in the Agnaya angle and eating materials almirah should be in the right hand side; by doing so the food will taste good.

(7) The bedsheet should be changed in the day time.

(8) The shoes & chappals should not be scattered; it gives birth to quarrel.

(9) The vegetable after cutting should not be kept on the floor but in the utensils, otherwise the taste of the vegetable would be absorbed by the floor.

(10) Never keep dirty clothes with washed clothes.

(11) If you do shaving then do it everyday otherwise keep long beard because uneven beard gives birth to poverty.

(12) There should not be useless photographs on the wall but only one or two important ones.

(13) Combs & Cosmetics should be kept decorated and at proper place.

(14) The towels should be kept away from the guests & outsiders.

(15) The photograhps of dead peaple should not be in the drawing room or near the doors.

(16) There should be a symbol of swastik or photographs of Ganesh-Lakshmi on the walls of doors of entrance.

(17) You should put one glass of water near the main door which will give prosperity.

(18) The clothes worn during the night should be changed before 8 O'clock in the morning.

(19) Expose your body to first rays of the Sun in the morning.

(20) Before the sun-rise you should clean your courtyard.

(21) While going for important work you should not see or eat egg or meat. But seeing or eating fish & curd is very lucky and auspicious.

(22) You should avoid fans with harsh noise which results in quarrel in the house all the day.

(23) Scents occupy an important place in a person's life. Our inner instincts get hold of scents immediately. So while sleeping or in the morning or evening one should apply scents. It is very peaceful.

This way we see that by obeying the Vaastu and its law we can live a peaceful & prosperous life.